Humility
AND THE ELEVATION OF THE MIND TO GOD

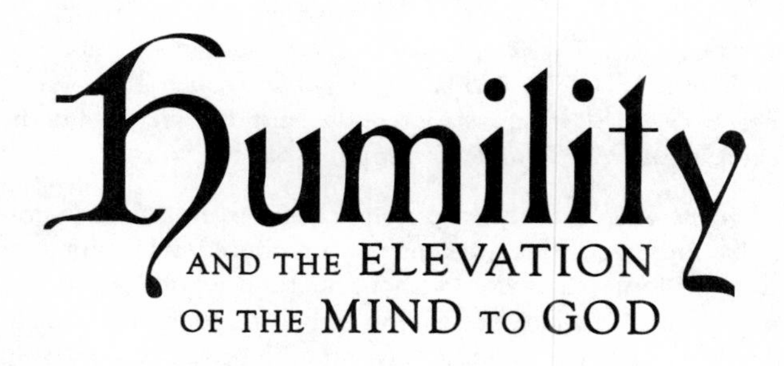

THOMAS À KEMPIS

Translated by
FR. ROBERT NIXON, OSB

TAN Books
Gastonia, North Carolina

Translated by Fr. Robert Nixon, OSB

This TAN Books English edition is translated from the Latin edition entitled *Opera Omnia Thomae à Kempis*, originally published in Antwerp in 1601. *The Life of the Venerable Thomas à Kempis* by Heribert Roswed, SJ, is a translation of the Latin text included in the 1654 edition of *De Imitatione Christi* published in Lyon.

Cover design by Caroline Green

Interior images: pg viii: Jesus and the Disciples on the Road to Emmaus, pg xii: Portrait of Thomas À Kempis (engraving), Look and Learn / Elgar Collection / Bridgeman Images, pg xxiv: The Sermon on the Mount, pg 12: Baruch Writes Jeremiah's Prophecies, and pg 46: The Annunciation. Images from The Holy Scriptures, Old and New Testaments books collection published in 1885, Stuttgart-Germany, engravings by Gustave Dore, images acquired from Nicku/Shutterstock.

ISBN: 978-1-5051-2234-3
Kindle ISBN: 978-1-5051-2235-0
ePUB ISBN: 978-1-5051-2236-7

Published in the United States by
TAN Books
PO Box 269
Gastonia, NC 28053
www.TANBooks.com

Printed in the United States of America

To the memory of John Moorehouse,
a wonderful and gifted herald of the Gospel and
dedicated servant of God, the Church, and humanity

CONTENTS

Jesus and the Disciples on the Road to Emmaus

TRANSLATOR'S INTRODUCTION

It is often said that, apart from the Bible, the most influential work of literature in the entire history of Christian spirituality is *The Imitation of Christ* by Thomas à Kempis (1380–1470). It has been a treasured source of inspiration and guidance for followers of Christ for over five hundred years and continues to attract a wide contemporary readership. Among those who were deeply devoted to it were Sir Thomas More, Henry VIII, St. Ignatius Loyola, John Wesley, St. Thérèse of Lisieux, Oscar Wilde, and countless others. There are known to be no less than two thousand editions of the work in existence.

Despite the popularity of *The Imitation of Christ*, it is not widely recognized that Thomas à Kempis was also the author of a great many other works in a variety of genres. Indeed, the complete Latin editions of his writings run to several weighty tomes. And many of his writings, especially his shorter works, remain untranslated.

This volume presents, for the first time in English, three short but wonderful spiritual works of this great author: *Humility*, *The Elevation of the Mind to God*, and a collection of *Devout Prayers.* In these writings, many of the themes of *The Imitation of Christ* are strongly evident, such as the practice of humility, self-denial, and resignation, modeled after the teaching and example of Jesus.

But other aspects of the author's personality are also exhibited. For example, in *The Elevation of the Mind to God,* the reader encounters a passionate and mystical yearning for a God who is utterly transcendent and eternal. In the *Devout Prayers,* there are many touching instances of affectionate and personal piety and devotion, especially to the Virgin Mary and other saints whom the author held particularly dear.

Included in this volume also is an early biography of Thomas written in 1597 by the important Jesuit scholar Heribert Rosweyd (1569–1629). This brief history offers a fascinating insight into a gifted and passionate man whose life was characterized by faith, humility, industry, and true dedication to the glory of God and the service of his neighbor.

The translations contained herein will certainly be of profound interest to all those who have been inspired or fascinated by the author's undoubted masterpiece, *The Imitation of Christ*. It is the hope of the present translator that these gentle and inspired writings, offered here in English for the first time, may prove edifying to all who peruse them and may generate further interest in the work of this revered and beloved spiritual author.

The humble translator,
Fr. Robert Nixon, OSB

Portrait of Thomas à Kempis

THE LIFE OF THE VENERABLE THOMAS À KEMPIS

by
Heribert Roswed, SJ

Thomas à Kempis was born in the village of Kempen, located in the diocese of Cologne, and it is from this place that he received his surname. His parents were Johannes and Gertrude. Considered from a worldly point of view, they were distinguished neither by noble lineage nor by wealth. Indeed, their nobility consisted solely in their piety, and their wealth in their probity of life. Yet they lived in a contented manner, supporting themselves by the labor of their hands. To this couple were born twin sons, Thomas and Johannes.

Johannes, named after his father, had been the first to be born. He undertook studies in the city of Deventer. Subsequently, he entered the Order of Canons Regular of the Congregation of Windesheim, joining the community at Mount St. Agnes in the municipality of Zwolle. Having commendably fulfilled various roles and offices for his community, Johannes was eventually to die there a peaceful and holy death.

Thomas was born in the year of the Lord 1380, during the pontificate of Urban VI and the reign of the Emperor Charles IV. After spending his first years with his parents, he was seen to be well suited to literary studies and took himself to Deventer for this purpose. At this time, he was no more than thirteen years of age. One of the factors that encouraged him in this endeavor was the fame of a certain learned priest, scholar, and teacher who resided there, Florentius, whose acquaintance he desired to make. This Florentius was the prefect of a distinguished house of studies. In fact, all manner of studies flourished at Deventer at that time, and it could truly be described then as the "Athens of Belgium."

Having arrived at Deventer, the first concern of Thomas was to meet with his twin brother, Johannes, who was already a student there, and to solicit his advice and guidance about what steps he should take. His brother recommended him to the renowned Florentius, who graciously accepted him into his establishment—known as the Brotherhood of Common Life—as a student. Thus Thomas, an affable youth of good habits, entered a fraternal community of men who were illustrious both for learning and piety, living and studying under the supervision of Florentius. Needless to say, he delighted in their companionship and profited greatly by their example. He exhibited himself as diligent in his duties within the community, assiduous in his studies, and devout in his prayer.

There, in the space of a few years, he progressed steadily in his academic accomplishments, and no less so in his piety. Indeed, the several volumes of spiritual writings that he authored during this time attest powerfully to this. These works are of such wonderful devotion and utility that they may never be sufficiently praised. While in this house of studies, he dedicated himself to the copying of many ancient manuscripts, thereby bringing considerable benefits to his fellow students and to the community.

From his boyhood, Thomas nourished a fervent attachment to the Blessed Virgin, and it was his custom to offer daily devotions to her. However, the piety of youth is seldom firm or stable, and in the course of time, he became somewhat less consistent in this practice. Sometimes, when he was busy or distracted, he would skip his daily devotions. Later, such omissions extended to two, three, or four days, and eventually even a week. Alas! Finally, he abandoned altogether his former custom of offering daily homage to the great Mother of God.

Then a vision came to him one night in a dream. He was standing in the lecture room with an assembly of other scholars. His master of studies, Florentius, was there also, and the students were listening attentively as he read to them the words of Scripture. Suddenly, Thomas beheld a cloud coming down from heaven on which stood Holy Mary, the Queen of heaven and earth. Though she was invisible to everyone else, Thomas saw her move around the room and embrace and kiss each of the students in turn with maternal love. He himself felt his devotion to her burn with renewed ardor. Joyfully, he waited for her to arrive at him, hoping and expecting to receive her gracious and kindly embrace.

But when the Mother of God arrived at him, she did not embrace him at all but instead reprimanded him bitterly. "You expect to receive my embrace? You, who neglect to pay me the honor you had once promised to me? Where have your customary devotions gone? Why have your prayers vanished, the homage which you formerly poured out to me with sighs and tears? Has your love for me grown cold and your ardor become dull? Why does your former piety vacillate thus? Depart from me! For you are surely unworthy of my embrace, since you have neglected such an easy thing as to offer a daily greeting to your beloved!"

And with these well-deserved admonitions having been pronounced, the Blessed Virgin disappeared into the heavens. Thomas, awakening from his slumber, then recognized his own failing. He immediately committed himself to the amendment of his ways. And, lest once more he should lose the embrace of the Mother of God, he resumed his former devotions and thenceforth did not allow one day of his life to pass by without offering his homage to the Blessed Virgin. O happy correction that renewed the bond of love and erased previous negligence by a fresh commitment!

While living in the Brotherhood of Common Life, he was often afflicted by various sufferings of soul and of body. In such cases, he would pray fervently before a crucifix placed upon his wall, expressing himself more by his tears than by his words.

After living for some seven years in the brotherhood, he felt a more determined vocation to consecrated life. Florentius encouraged this vocation strongly, and in 1399, Thomas went to the house of the Canons Regular at Mount St. Agnes near the city of Zwolle. At this time, this community was but a small and obscure one. He took with him a letter of recommendation from his former teacher, Florentius. His brother, Johannes, had entered the same house some years previously and now occupied the position of prior there. He was received readily and with great delight and fraternal affection in accordance with the words of the psalmist: "Behold, how good and how pleasant it is for brethren to dwell together in unity!"[1]

As a candidate for consecrated life and sacred orders, he was fervid and enthusiastic in his vocation, yet without any trace of temerity or presumption. After five years in initial formation, he received the habit of religious life, and in the following year, he bound himself to the consecrated life by solemn vows. He was outstanding in his piety, his obedience to his superiors, and his charity and benevolence towards his confreres.

---

1 Psalm 133:1.

He never gave rein to idleness, which is truly the font of all evil. Rather, he constantly devoted himself to reading or copying sacred books, both for the common use of the community and his own education. Indeed, he spent much of the night—the time between Matins and Lauds—occupied in this manner. This was done, of course, not without taking its toll upon his physical vigor and mental energies. Out of the books he copied in this manner, there remains in existence a complete Bible, a missal, and many of the writings of St. Bernard of Clairvaux. These superb manuscripts attest both to the artistry of his penmanship and the magnitude of his industry.

In liturgical prayers within the oratory and the church, Thomas exhibited a degree of reverence and spiritual presence which almost exceeds description. Whenever he chanted the psalms, his face was raised towards the heavens, and he was observed to be captured and seized beyond himself by the very sweetness of the psalmody. It was as if he escaped the bounds of the material world and his soul flew into the celestial realms! Indeed, it was only the toes of his feet which maintained contact with the earth, while all his other members were transported upwards. He would always chant the psalms standing erect, never sitting nor resting on a bench or stool. And he was always the first to enter the oratory for prayer, and always the last to leave.

Such was the visible delight and enthusiastic animation he displayed in singing the psalms that one of his confreres, making an amusing pun, commented, "Thomas savors these psalms as if he were eating fine salmon!"[2] Now, the salmon is indeed a most delectable fish to eat. Thomas replied to his confrere's jocular observation with the following pithy retort:

The salmon is a wondrous fish;
Well cooked, it is a tasty dish.
But, if consumed without due care
Can health, and even life, impair.

And thus the psalms, if sung with heart,
All joys of heaven shall impart;
But if with spirits dull they're read
Can leave one's soul dismayed and dead.

The conversation of Thomas always pertained to God and Sacred Scripture. Even in the presence of important people, if the discussion concerned only worldly

---

2 There is a pun being made here between the word for *psalm* and *salmon.*

matters, he would be silent, as if he were mute or without the capacity for speech. He would not respond, nor would he ask anything, unless some unavoidable necessity compelled him to do so. He much preferred to be seen as entirely ignorant and dull in such matters. However, if the conversation was about God and divine mysteries, his discourse was like a ceaseless river of words, flowing forth with miraculous beauty and crystalline clarity. Whenever he was asked about such things, he would never fail to give a comprehensive and enlightening reply. Nevertheless, it was his practice in such matters always to take some moments for meditation and reflection before answering.

Such was his remarkable eloquence and accomplishment in speech that he quickly became widely renowned as an orator, preacher, and conversationalist. Many would travel from distant cities and regions to visit his community, drawn by the desire of hearing the wonderful words of Thomas.

His brethren were constantly filled with admiration and amazement at the imperturbable patience of Thomas in tolerating adversities and difficulties of all kinds. He not only mildly and benignly tolerated the vices and shortcomings of others but even kindly made excuses for them as much as he possibly could.

Throughout his life, he always displayed exemplary temperance, moderation, modesty, and humility. His care in providing for the needs of others was diligent and indefatigable, and his enthusiasm for the cultivation of the liturgy and the beautification of the oratory and church was unbounded. Yet he viewed all things, except those pertaining to God and to true religion, as mere vanities and passing shadows. Indeed, his detachment from worldly vanities and mundane business was such that the mere mention of them was apt to fill him with tedium and distraction.

Thomas was so greatly enamored of sacred reading and the solitude of his monastic cell that he formulated a kind of personal motto expressing this love. This he frequently repeated verbally and would inscribe in his books. It read thus: "In all things I have sought rest. But I have found it nowhere, except in hidden corners and in books!"

His mercy and kindness was such that while still a young man, he was chosen as subprior of his community. Afterwards, he was elevated to the position of procurator, or domestic prefect. Although he performed these duties with all diligence, the primary calling of his heart remained that of divine contemplation and prayerful studies. For this reason, he was soon relieved of these onerous offices and returned to his former role of subprior. This role he fulfilled creditably for a great many years.

In stature, he was rather below average height but of muscular build. His complexion was ruddy and somewhat swarthy. His vision was most acute, so that he never had recourse to the aid of spectacles or other such devices, even as he approached his final days.

When Thomas had meritoriously completed seventy-one years of religious life at Mount St. Agnes with great fruitfulness to his community, he was called by the Lord to the Mount of Eternity. Indeed, he had long contemplated his return to his heavenly homeland with the most fervent longing and joyful anticipation. His blessed soul, departing from the earthly dwelling place of his mortal body, ascended to the eternal tabernacle of heaven to enjoy there the wonderful vision of God forever. He died peacefully in the ninety-second year of his mortal life, in the year of our Lord 1470, on the twenty-fifth day of July.

The Sermon on the Mount

HUMILITY

A commendation of humility, which is the foundation of all virtues

I

"Learn from me, for I am meek and humble of heart,"[1] says the Lord. Our highest teacher and lawgiver, Jesus Christ, urged us to learn the virtue of humility. For whoever cultivates this marvelous virtue will quickly arrive at spiritual perfection. But without humility, no amount of study of Sacred Scripture or theology, nor any efforts at good works are able to achieve anything lasting. In vain are all our labors unless they are accompanied by humility.

The very first lesson of Christ is, therefore, humility of heart; for this is the foundation of all virtues and

---

1 Matthew 11:29.

indispensable to the attainment of eternal salvation. Whoever desires to receive grace now and eternal life in the world to come should, therefore, study Christ's lesson and example of humility with diligence. But whoever neglects humility will lose any benefits their good thoughts and works would otherwise have gained them.

It behooves each Christian soul to meditate carefully on the teachings of Christ. This includes all religious, all priests, all bishops, all servants, all nobles, all commoners, all the educated, and all the simple. And Christ teaches us humility, not pride. He teaches us useful things, not vanities. He teaches what is true, not what is false; what is heavenly, not what is earthly.

II

Any person who imitates the example of Christ will quickly become wise and happy. Humility was a particular virtue of Christ; it is therefore feared by the devil and despised by the world. But those who hold it firmly in their hearts are pleasing to God and his angels. Such people will have a secure and blessed passage from this world to the next in accordance with Christ's words, "Blessed are the poor in spirit, for theirs is the kingdom of heaven."[2]

---

2 Matthew 5:3.

Without humility, there is neither salvation nor real virtue. Nor can any action done without humility be pleasing to God. Any work or deed—no matter how noble or persevering—achieves nothing for the soul if it is motivated or accompanied by pride and arrogance.

Profound humility is a stronghold of all the virtues and triumphs over all their enemies. The one to whom humility is granted shall exult in the grace of Christ. For it makes a person like the Lord's intimate friend, who will willingly and joyfully submits himself to whatever Divine Providence determines. The truly humble person ascribes all good things he does to his Creator and is willing to resign himself in all imaginable situations.

But without humility, any aspirations or pretensions to sanctity remain empty and fruitless. External piety and uprightness mean nothing unless accompanied by internal humility. While humility is a ladder ascending to the highest blessedness, its absence can easily cast the soul down to hell. An example of this is to be found in the parable of the humble and contrite tax-collector and the proud and presumptuous Pharisee.[3] Call to mind and be horrified at the fate of Lucifer, who in his pride was cast out of heaven. Consider the humble

---

[3] See Luke 18:9–14.

poor man, Lazarus, who was taken up by the angels to rejoice in the bosom of Abraham.[4]

Thus it was that the Blessed Virgin Mary, the Mother of Jesus, proclaimed in her wondrous canticle, "He has cast down the mighty from their thrones, and exalted the lowly."[5] There are, indeed, a vast multitude of examples of this in Sacred Scripture, aside from those mentioned above. For new spiritual perils arise daily for all those who grow proud because of their imagined virtue or strength.

III

The person who is intent upon gaining the approval of others and being thought of as great becomes more and more distant from God. And such people pass away like the vanishing smoke or fading shadows.

Everyone who is proud becomes impure in the sight of God. Proud people do not truly know themselves, nor do they perceive their own calling, condition, and destiny clearly. The more pride raises up one's own self-estimation, the more liable one becomes to the judgment of God. The one who climbs high in pride, raises himself up for an inevitable fall. The humble

---

4 See Luke 16:19–31.

5 Luke 1:52.

person, however, who keeps his feet firmly planted on the ground, will stand securely.

Hidden pride is a most pernicious vice, the more so since it is not recognized and does not recognize itself. On the outside, it may appear gentle, mild, and even humble. Yet inside, it burns away bitterly. The person who is subject to such pride becomes inordinately elated when he is successful but is disturbed and dejected in the face of adversity or failure.

The one who seeks to condemn others and justify himself ends up condemning himself by displaying his pride and arrogance. It is typical of a proud person to seek to please himself and to trust entirely in his own opinions. Such people are often quick to criticize others and to deride those who seem simple to them.

But the proud position themselves so that they are liable to fall into dangerous delusions, errors, and adversity. For it reflects a distorted and perverse sense of judgment to think always well of oneself but to be hasty to think ill of others.

IV

Pride is difficult to overcome except through enduring much suffering, performing menial duties, and facing difficult and desperate situations. The person who finds it difficult to obey the instructions or directions of another is very far from true humility. But humility is the precious root of all virtues. It readily brings forth the fruit of obedience, which soon ripens into the flower of charity.

The truly humble person is honestly aware of his own weaknesses and failings. He judges himself more strictly than he judges others and regrets his wrongdoings and sins constantly and sincerely.

The humble person does not readily judge his superiors and those positioned above him, lest he incur the judgment of God himself. He does not perturb or vex his peers and equals. Rather, he honors the seniors, tolerates those who exhibit shortcomings, prays for those who are tempted, and helps those who are in need.

When two humble people are associated together, they will always get along well with each other. But when two proud people are associated together, they will compete with each other and dissentions will inevitably arise. The truly humble person may be safely praised, for—regardless of the praise and the recognition of his merits—he remains mindful of his fragility and weaknesses. Moreover, he does not forget that the eyes of God are upon him at all times, observing his thoughts and actions, and even every movement of his heart.

V

It is a very useful practice to train oneself in humility. It is wise to fear the unseen judgment of God and to think often about one's final end. It is characteristic of a truly humble person not to be greatly affected by human praise. For the one who is intent upon heavenly glory will not consider earthly glory as something of any great consequence.

In contrast, the person who seeks to be praised and glorified during this life will never be firmly established in the truth. Such a person, who is intent upon human praise and approval, cannot genuinely love God above all else, or will—at best—love God with only a divided heart.

Those in positions of authority who remain humble are particularly dear to God and will receive fitting honor from him. The one who is subject to others, and accepts this humbly, will be crowned with a great reward in heaven. The person who is sober and chaste becomes a companion to the angels and is an adornment to the human race. And the one who flees from the tumult of worldly activities will make steady progress in chastity and self-control.

The devout person loves and cultivates times of solitude so that he may contemplate God more freely and intently. The monk who is silent and given to constant prayer shall walk with God and penetrate the mysteries of heaven. The one who does good works and endures injustices patiently will gather wonderful fruit for himself in the future.

But the person who is occupied with considering subtle and sophisticated questions and problems, and so neglects the virtue of humility, digs a pit for himself into which he will surely fall. The one who ambitiously aspires to a lofty and exalted position in this world climbs a perilous scaffold, which may serve as a lethal gallows for the soul.

The prudent person, however, does nothing rashly or on impulse. The faithful person will neglect nothing pertaining to virtue and morals and will not commit any deceit. People who are truly just examine all the causes of a matter and all its circumstances before offering any judgment. But almost all of us are deceived at times by merely apparent goodness and false and specious righteousness.

VI

The one who trusts too much in his own opinions and judgments exposes himself to grave perils. It is generally wiser to defer to those who are more experienced and more knowledgeable. To seek the advice and the prayers of others is a sure sign of humility.

Often, indeed, God speaks to us through the words of another person. And he may tell us, by this means, things he has not revealed directly. The perfection of humility and obedience is displayed by one who is ready to hear the voice of God even through an inexpert person or by one who replies to any angry person with mildness. Obedience is due to all legitimately constituted superiors. The one who is truly humble will obey even in trivial or difficult matters.

What benefits the spirit most of all is conscious acts of profound humility. The person who deliberately overcomes his own preferences, desires, or opinions also overcomes thereby the enemy of the soul. For humility is indeed the most powerful weapon against the wiles of the devil.

What is so rare and marvelous as the person who does admirable things, yet who still views himself with humility? When this happens, it is not the result of any personal effort or merit but purely the freely-given grace of God.

VII

In this life, the hazards and attacks of the devil assail us both from right and from left, from both the outside world and from within our own hearts. There is no more powerful weapon against these hazards and attacks than true humility and devout prayer made with a pure conscience. With each proud thought that enters the mind and with every haughty sentiment that springs up in the heart, the soul encounters a new snare or trap.

A humble person does not become proud when he finds something good or meritorious in his thoughts or actions. Rather, he recognizes it as a gift from God and gives sincere thanks for the grace he has received.

The person who humbles himself acts wisely and judiciously and avoids a great many dangers. Humility helps obtain forgiveness for our shortcomings and helps to reconcile us to God; it builds up our neighbor, it frustrates the devil, it opens heaven to the sinner, and it purges away all sins. But many souls become deceived and dejected through the illusions of pride and so end up stumbling badly.

Be humble, therefore, and always be mindful of your own lowliness, recalling your weaknesses and failings—lest you should fall a prey to the devil and so become displeasing to God. For the kingdom of heaven receives no one except for the truly humble, and the Lord chooses none but those free from presumption and pride. Indeed, God withholds his approval even from the righteous unless their righteousness is founded upon and accompanied by the wonderful and Christlike virtue of genuine humility.

Baruch Writes Jeremiah's Prophecies

THE ELEVATION OF THE MIND TO GOD

"Be still and know that I am God."[1]

I seek you, my God, but not through any of the senses of my body or through any perceptible images. Rather, I turn within myself, to the interior chamber of my thoughts and feelings, and the realm which lies beyond all thoughts and feelings. For there, O Lord, you illuminate my heart and mind. You are, indeed, the eternal truth, the immeasurable goodness, the incomprehensible brilliance exceeding all created things, ungraspable by the mind alone and transcending all celestial powers. According to the mystery of your divine nature, you remain unknown and unknowable.

---

1 Psalm 46:10.

And yet, through pure grace, you communicate yourself to holy souls, manifesting something of the infinite glory of your heavenly nature, which entirely exceeds time, space, thought, and imagination.

O blessed Trinity, one and only God—Father, Son, and Holy Spirit! You are the eternal glory and highest beatitude of all the saints and the epitome and perfection of all heavenly powers. From you, through you, and in you alone do all things come into being, exist, and reach their end. Make known to me your ways, O Lord, and teach me your paths; for all your ways are beautiful and all your paths are of peace. You have declared that "blessed are the pure of heart" and "blessed are the peace-makers."[2] These two counsels guide us on the pathways that lead to the blessings of the contemplative life.

Let us work and pray diligently, therefore, so that our hearts may be rendered pure from every stain of sin. And then the way which shall lead us to God—in whom all our happiness and peace abides—shall be made open to us.

---

[2] Matthew 5:8–9.

A prayer that the mind may be freed from its bondage to the things of the physical senses

I earnestly beseech you, my God, and pray to you from the very depths of my being. Free me, and rescue my soul—which is currently distracted and held captive by all kinds of earthly cares, worries, and desires. By the radiance of your enlightenment, may I discover you within myself, O God; for truly, you fashioned me in your own divine, precious, and incorruptible image.

Indeed, the beauty and likeness of your supreme wisdom does not shine forth in any created thing in the world as much as it does in the human soul. You made the human soul alone with the capacity to know and to love you, and, through the gift of reason, placed it above all other things in creation. Lord, raise up my mind from all earthly concerns and purify the affection of my heart! Renew me according to the "interior human" which you lovingly created. Repair your divine image within me, through the seven-fold grace of the Holy Spirit. Truly you have made the human soul as something immortal, invisible, and incorporeal, capable of receiving the eternal Truth, uniquely blessed with reason and self-awareness, and for this reason surpassing all other living things. On account of this reason and self-awareness, it is more worthy than any visible or perceptible thing to bear the image of God.

O Lord, remove and expel from me whatever is able to stain or darken your image, lest it should become unworthy of your kindly gaze and offend the eyes of your majesty. Deign to renew this most precious and noble image of yourself, which is within me, by the power of your love. Illuminate your image within me with the gift of your intelligence and visit it without ceasing. For, in your omnipotence, it is you alone who hold it in being, and in your omniscience, you perceive and comprehend it always and in full.

Recall, O Lord, how you created my soul *from* nothing but not *for* nothing. Remember how you redeemed it from the chains of sin by the awesome and sacred exchange of your holy cross. Do not let this same soul which you created and redeemed, O Lord, be conquered by earthly vices but defend it from all evil and enrich it with your grace. Multiply within it the gifts of your generosity that it may always know the abundance of your saving power.

O God, you alone are my Truth and my mercy! Grant that I may see that which lies beyond the circumscribed world of physical forms, to perceive without material images, and to gaze with an illumination exceeding that of any created light. Grant me the ability to seek with the intelligence of a truly clean mind, for you promise that you shall be beheld by those who are pure of heart.[3] This is indeed a stupendous and amazing promise! And yet it is perfectly congruous with true purity and illumination. For those who have left behind all earthly concerns and transcended all physical realities shall deservedly merit to contemplate the hidden light of eternal truth. The more such minds withdraw from the created light and from the things of this world, the more they shall be seized and raised above their individual selfhood to enter into the secret realm of the divine splendor. And how magnificent shall be that vision; how pure that perception! How blessed that eye shall be which beholds the Truth without physical senses or comprehensible images of any kind, O God!

It behooves the human heart to be free and purged from all disordered attachments. It behooves the mind to be undistracted by the tumult and flurry of the individual things of this world if it wishes to comprehend the entirety of the universe by virtue of the eternal and limitless light of Divinity. Grant, O Lord, that in

---

3 See Matthew 5:8.

your light, I may see light.[4] The light for which my soul longs is not the light of the heavens above, nor the light of the earth; nor is it the light of the angels or the light of human beings. Rather, it is the eternal light—uncreated, infinite, ineffable, incomprehensible and surpassing all existence and conception.

But how heavy is the weight of the physical reality, which weighs me down! How burdensome is the law of sin, which seems to dwell within me. This so often draws me away from the contemplation of the celestial light, from the face of the glory of God, and from the sweet taste of eternal joy. It distracts me from the entrance into the heavenly city of the souls of the blessed, who are surrounded and filled with unending happiness. O God, grant your grace and heavenly blessing to me, your lowly servant.

Of course, I am not yet worthy to drink from the spring of living waters, which flows forth into eternal life. But, please, visit me frequently, most merciful Jesus, and in your love, help me to raise myself above all earthly distractions and lower realities and to see you alone. For you are the one, eternal goodness. Let me seek you above all else and love you completely for your sake alone.

---

4 Cf. Psalm 35:9.

The uncreated, eternal, and boundless Word of God, which illuminates the soul more than anything else

"Your word is a lamp for my feet and a light for my path."[5] O Word of God, most high and exalted, surpassing and transcending all else! You illuminate all things, leading them towards perfection and leaving nothing in creation in darkness. Your Word, O Lord, is my light and the joy of my soul. Without it, I would languish in the darkness of sorrow, but with it, I am filled with joy and light. Open to me, Lord, the door of your eternal radiance so that I may find your divine Word in the heavens. For it is in heaven that your Word eternally abides and "your truth lasts from age to age."[6]

How wondrous the eternal Word, which exceeds all measure and bounds! Through it, all things were made and all things are renewed, in infinite wisdom and perfect justice! The very heights of the heavens cannot hold this Word. The depths of the abyss tremble before it, and the breadth of the earth cannot attain to it. This eternal Word of God cannot be communicated, even by a multitude of human words. Nor can it be

---

5 Psalm 118:105.

6 Psalm 118:142.

depicted by images or comprehended by any mortal intellect. Rather, it is beyond all that can be described and imagined.

Nevertheless, it is able to be believed in and loved, despite the fact that it cannot be comprehended or expressed. For the Word of God is God himself, as testifies the blessed evangelist John: "In the beginning was the Word, and the Word was with God and the Word was God."[7]

O, how ineffable and adorable is this Word of God! How sweet it is to hear, how blissful to meditate upon, how blessed to enjoy! This Word speaks to the soul in a multiplicity of ways—through the Scriptures, through angels, through prophecies, and through secret revelations. Yet it is much more sublime when it communicates itself directly and silently to the faithful mind as the absolute but entirely transcendent truth.

How much I wish that I were able to taste and see the sweetness of this divine Word! It is the light of the soul, the life of the living, and the happiness of those reigning in heaven. With it, no pressure of work would ever crush me, nor any temptation from earthly things would ever hold me back. Indeed, I would quickly

---

7 John 1:1.

overcome all obstacles and allurements of this world. O how good it is to cling to God, to enjoy his Word, to live and think according to this Word, and so to come to await its immortal fruits!

It is, indeed, not a word which is produced or transmitted by sound or conceived in the imagination or intellect, but rather it exceeds all spoken utterance and all powers of imagination and thought. For human words arise and quickly pass away, whereas the Word of God endures eternally. Remaining unchanged in itself, it works changes in all things. In all human and earthly matters, there is always a before and an after. Their existence is therefore never perfect and complete but only transitory and temporary. It is the one God, who alone is eternally existent, who possesses true being. And it is this God, the source of all existence, who imparts goodness to each created thing according to its proper nature and graciously preserves all things in being.

O unique Word of God! This Word was not created in time but was eternally begotten by the Father and, in the realm of time, was made incarnate through the Blessed Virgin Mary! O eternal Word of God, immense and infinite, the bread of angels and of humans. This bread, when it is taken, is not reduced nor transformed into the one who consumes it. Rather, it transforms the one who consumes it, drawing them from the realm of created things up to the incomprehensible and eternal Good. O, what a marvelous thing it is to know this Word of God! What a stupendous wonder it is to hear this Word—the Word not of any human being, nor of any angel, nor of any created being existing under heaven, but of God himself! This Word dwells forever in the bosom of the Father, and yet from there proceeds forth as the only begotten Son, coeternal and coequal with the Father in divinity and power.

Who is able to comprehend or know this eternal Word except through the utterances of this Word itself? For he said, whilst abiding in the flesh, "No one knows the Son except the Father, and no one knows the Father except the Son, and those to whom the Son wishes to reveal him."[8] There is, therefore, a need for a revelation made by the power and grace of this Word in order that this same Word may be received and understood. Accordingly, the prophet David prayed, "Grant to me understanding, that I may live."[9]

For the life and salvation of the soul is to hear this Word, to love it, and to place all one's hopes in it. The faithful soul desires to enjoy this Word always. But it is

---

8 Matthew 11:27.

9 Psalm 118:144.

not granted to perceive it nor to experience it except by the will and gracious self-revelation of the Word itself, which is Christ. The soul is able to strive and able to desire by its own efforts, yet it is not able to comprehend nor receive the Word unless the Word wills to reveal itself through grace and the spirit.

My soul, prepare yourself as best you are able! Make yourself ready! Abide in solitude and shun the tumult of the vices. Let not anything exterior to yourself disturb or distract you. Let nothing cause you to become troubled. Inflamed with love of the Highest Good, cultivate detachment from all passing things. Turn yourself from the external world to the inner chamber of your heart. Direct your thoughts and sighs to what lies in the heavens. Raise yourself above yourself! Transcend all things which exist in the realms of time and space and leave behind every created reality.

Strive to separate your heart from all limited and conditional things, even those of the most lofty grade. By doing this shall you find the uncreated Word, which is infinitely exalted above all creation. You will be able to do this precisely as much as the Word itself shall help you. As much as it illuminates you, that much shall you see. As much as it inspires and inflames you, so much will you burn with love.

In this invincible and immortal Word, you shall truly conquer the world and all its perils and snares and shall prevail against each and every foe and adversity! In this Word, you shall stand strong and unwavering in all virtues. For the sake of this Word, you shall gladly leave all things—father, mother, friend, and neighbors. That is to say, you shall safely overcome all temptations and allurements of flesh and blood. Ultimately, you shall indeed become one spirit with this Word. You shall come to desire and wish for nothing else—in small things and in great, in present affairs or future realities—except for that which is pleasing to this divine and eternal Truth, which is nothing other than the will of God. It is for the sake of knowing and loving this uncreated Word, who is with God and who *is* God, that all the writings of Scripture and all the teachings of the saints have come to us.

The saints of God have said and written many great and magnificent things. Yet all of these writings and teachings reach only to the extent that it can be granted to mere mortals to grasp the divine Word and its mysteries. In its own perfect and ultimate nature, it remains ever and wholly ineffable and incomprehensible. Every holy and inspired word proceeds from the illumination of this eternal Word. For this is the unique font and exemplar of all that is true, good, and holy. In it is all virtue, power, wisdom, and intelligence.

By means of external and comprehensible signs and teachings, it communicates to us the journey whereby we may seek and find its eternal Truth. Since, as creatures, we may not comprehend the Creator directly, we are granted comprehensible, visible, and perceptible manifestations of the Divinity, including Sacred Scripture, to lead us forth. But we should never be satisfied by such external signs or by mere audible or written words, no matter how beautiful and profound they may be. Rather, we are called always to seek earnestly within the unspoken and hidden depths of our own heart and to strive longingly towards the glorious, celestial, and utterly transcendent kingdom hidden above us. For there we shall find the one, perfect, and eternal Good, which is God himself. It is this infinite yet unseen Goodness that nourishes the splendid hosts of angels and teaches all the faithful with the rich eloquence of sacred doctrine. And, whenever it wills, it sends forth the sacred radiance of internal illumination, whereby it grants to the devout mind the grace of sensing those divine realities which exceed all the powers of sense and reason.

On the ardent desire which inflames the soul when it has been visited by the Word of God, its unique and beloved Spouse

"O Lord, all that I long for is known to you, and my tears and sighs are not hidden from your sight."[10] Lord, my soul longs for the bliss of eternity above all else. When I recall this blessed eternity and the celestial glory of heaven, my own actions seem burdensome to me. Whatever I perceive in earthly things strikes me with tedium and languor. The usual human consolations do not delight me at all. I can find no remedy for the aching longing of my heart, unless by being perfectly united with you, O God.

Thus it is you, my beloved Lord, who are the cause of my pain! You are the author of my languor and the unbearable heat of my love. You have wounded me with the hidden darts of desire, igniting my soul and penetrating the very depths of my heart. Shall you cruelly abandon me now to wallow in my affliction and to mourn with fervent, unfulfilled longing? Why do you flee from me so hastily into the remote and inaccessible regions of opaque darkness into which I am completely unable to follow?

---

10 Psalm 37:9.

O God, my holy Love, do not disdain one who longs for you so desperately! Do not conceal yourself from the vision of one who loves you sincerely. Rather, grant mercy to the soul that seeks you, and come quickly! For without you, I can neither live nor even exist.

Lord, even if you wish to subject me to trial and to test me, do not hesitate to do so. Do to me whatever pleases your will! But do not withhold the sweetness of your grace and mercy.

Grant, O Lord, that I may find grace in your sight, and kindly deign to include me amongst the multitude of your chosen. Abandon me not to the darkness—let not the weight of sorrow crush me utterly. Rather, kindly extend your right hand so that I may be saved, and let the light of your mercy shine forth and fill my soul.

A prayer for detachment from all earthly things

Lord Jesus Christ, you alone are my hope and my refuge. You are my best solace in times of trouble and my trusted guide in times of perplexity and uncertainty. Therefore, today, I renounce all things in this passing world for the sake of your love. I earnestly aspire to fulfill this resolution to the honor and glory of your holy name. I shall henceforth prefer your love to all my other attachments, whether to friends, parents, relatives, or all those who are dear to my heart.

> I renounce all earthly property, all castles,
> lands, mountains and valleys.
> I renounce all the rivers and flowing
> streams, the fields and meadows, the
> verdant woods and towering forests.
> I renounce all the beautiful buildings and
> majestic edifices raised up by human
> hands.
> I renounce all instruments of music, all flutes,
> harps and lyres, and every melody known
> to mortals.
> I renounce the rose, the orchid, the lotus, the
> lily, and every terrestrial flower, together
> with all their sweet and varied fragrances.
> I renounce all jokes, feasts, festivities, conversations, discussions, rumors and gossip.
> I renounce all riches, all cares, and all dignities.
> O Lord, I renounce for the sake of your love
> everything that can tempt and bind my
> soul, everything that can distract it,
> and render it impure and divided.

Yes, today I choose you, O God, as my protector! Govern and direct my life and provide for all of my needs. Console me in all sorrows and afflictions, and give me strength in my labors, together with the wisdom and fortitude to resist temptations. Let your grace assist me in everything I must do and undergo, for the sake of love of you and for the sake of the salvation of my soul.

> O God, you are my true home, my refuge and my fortress.
> You are my food, my drink, and my rest.
> You are my beloved companion, my truest friend.
> You are my brother and sister, my Father and patron.
> You are the shepherd and guardian of my life.

To you, O Lord, I therefore commend all that I am and all that I have. For apart from you, there is no salvation. Without you, there is no life. "May your mercy come upon me, O Lord."[11] May your grace be my constant companion. May your vigilant eye keep watch over me day and night. May your all-powerful hand protect

---

11 Psalm 33:22.

me from the foes and perils which threaten both from the right and from the left. Lead me along the right path, O Lord, into the celestial dwelling place of your infinite glory. There, let me praise and bless your holy name for ages unending. Amen.

A prayer for progress and perseverance in the virtues

O God, most holy Lord and Father, you direct, govern and weigh all things in due and proper measure. Accordingly, you seek, above all, that rational creatures should offer to you the love, honor, and service which is justly due to you. I therefore beseech that you direct my actions and deeds to be pleasing to you. Help me to restrain and overcome all movements of my heart or soul which are rebellious or contrary to your eternal will. Order all my affections so that I may reject whatever is evil and strive after all that is truly good. Help me to learn to contemplate and love you without relying upon the physical senses and the fleshly imagination.

Fortify and make firm my heart so that I may not be enslaved to earthly and exterior things but may seek fervently the things which are above. Nourish in me an unflagging desire for eternal realities and an aspiration to attain to the higher virtues and the enjoyment of celestial beatitude. In doing this, O Lord, your own honor shall be increased and I myself shall make progress upon my pilgrimage to happiness.

Let not the footstep of pride approach me, and let the plague of vainglory not menace me. Let me not be deceived by the manifold illusions of Satan, nor seized by any tempting and beguiling sweetness of mind, body, or spirit. Neither let me indulge in misguided private devotions which separate me from the Church and my community; nor let me vainly undertake excessive works of piety and penance, which serve to break the soul rather than to strengthen it.

Grant me, O Lord, to do nothing without discretion and prudence, and to have the humility to seek wise counsel in all matters. Direct my works and my prayer so that they may be offered with holy fear and reverence for your Divine Majesty. May I act with purity and freedom of heart, not swayed by passions and attachment to corruptible things. Grant to me a humble and quiet spirit, one that is never uncontrolled or garrulous. Let my soul adhere to no created being or object with any sinful attachment.

Rather, let my heart be pure and tranquil and affix itself to you alone. May my mind strive always after heaven and ever be secretly intent upon you, O God. In the midst of this passing world, let me know myself to be merely a pilgrim and to look upon all earthly things with a wise and judicious detachment.

Help me to perform all my actions and works in the exterior world in a manner which is fitting to the time and place and without detriment to my interior life. May all the works and labor which I undertake for your sake, O Lord, lead me and assist me in arriving at blessed contemplation. Indeed, let me do all things for your love and for the greater glory of your name, whether they are actions in the exterior world or prayers and thoughts within my heart. May I be given a spirit of prompt and mild resignation to carry all the burdens of this present life which you determine for me or my vocation requires of me. In this way, let me commend my whole being—body and soul—entirely to you, my Creator, with complete faith, trust, and obedience.

And remember me, O God, in the hour of my death. At that time, deal gently with me, your devoted servant; for it is not in my own merits but rather in your compassion and mercy that I place all my trust.

An exhortation made to the soul for humility and compunction

O my soul, submit yourself humbly and unresistingly to the will of God. For the sake of God, submit and resign yourself to all things and events of this created realm. Strive to think of yourself as the least of all things, and hold yourself unworthy even of the light itself. Recall that you have, by sin, offended God and his saints. Often, indeed, you have failed in your duty of due reverence.

Flee, O soul, to the refuge of tears, and implore heaven's mercy with great contrition of heart! Beg God to forgive you and treat you with mercy for anything you have done that is contrary to his divine and immeasurable kindness.

Before the final day of this mortal life and the dark horror of death arrives, with tears and prayers, strive to reconcile yourself to the face of your merciful Creator. Commit yourself each day to changing your life for the better so that, little by little, you may arrive at true sanctity.

A prayer for obtaining true and tearful contrition for sins

O God of all forgiveness, your nature is pure goodness itself, and all your works are mercy! Grant to me, according to the vastness of your compassion, perfect and complete contrition for my sins. Grant that I may weep the bitter tears of true penitence for all my sins and offenses so that I may be able to wash away the stain of guilt and purge my soul of its iniquity. Doing thus, may I merit to partake in the complete forgiveness of sins which you alone can grant, O Lord, so that I may rest securely in your compassion and take blessed refuge in your saving mercy!

Arm me with a holy zeal for justice so that I may rise up against even the worst of sinners and be on guard against all the thieves and bandits who lie in hiding around me. For I have indeed gravely offended you, my God, the Creator of heaven and earth. I have sinned not only in what I have done but also in what I have failed to do; for often have I neglected to offer due honor and glory to you, O Lord.

In such things, I have really been stealing from myself by taking away from the multitude of treasures you have stored away for me to enjoy in the future life.

I have inflicted grave wounds upon my own soul with the spears of sin. It is as if I have even been striving to kill my own spirit by being mastered by the temptations of the flesh.

O Lord my God, most just judge of all the universe, bestow upon me true contrition and sorrow for my sins, as much as you know that I truly deserve. Correct me and castigate me in this present life, Lord. For it is infinitely better for me that you freely punish me now than that you reserve the condemnation and retribution due to me for the future and final judgment. O loving and clement God, be merciful to me, though I am entirely unworthy and the greatest of all sinners. For you once deigned to enter this world for the sake of sinners. And in order to achieve their reconciliation, you accepted condemnation to the most fearful death and, filled with divine love, were crucified as the price of humanity's redemption.

A prayer for the attainment of love of virtue and abhorrence of vice

O God, you are the Lord of all virtues and their perfection and consummation. Place into my heart that virtue which is best of all—namely, the fervent love of your most sweet name. Plant in me the roots of true virtue and the seeds of holy meditation. Make this spring up and grow with the abundant greenness of good works. Let me not be a barren tree, which stands in your garden without producing anything of value. Rather, cultivate me so that I become like the fruitful olive tree. Whatever you find in me of vice, pull out by its very roots and leave not the slightest trace of it behind.

Give to me, O Lord, abhorrence of all my vices, great and small. Grant victory over my restless passions and mortification of my lustful desires. Grant control over every movement of pride, extinction of envy, mitigation of anger, expulsion of harmful melancholy, contempt for vainglory, flight from visible honors, and complete detachment from all earthly consolations.

Let me not be swayed, seduced, or captured by anything earthly, or vain, or ephemeral, or false, or deceptive, or empty, or futile. Render my heart impervious to the temptations of deceptive pleasures which appear sweet, and make it resilient in the face of all that seems hard or daunting.

Grant that I not be deceived or ensnared by any passing reality—which are, after all, but fleeting shadows. Fill my heart with desire for that which is eternal and love of that which is genuinely good. May I seek to attain every virtue and to grasp the highest truth of the Divinity so that I may at last arrive at everlasting beatitude. Grant to me a blessed and happy hour for my mortal death, and until then, grant that I walk constantly in fear and love of you, O Lord.

Cleanse my heart from every inordinate attachment to created things and from all that is able to impede or darken the way of my life's pilgrimage. May I be simple, pure, and sincerely and completely intent upon you, my God. Share with me something of the grace of your perfect, divine peace so that I may hold within my heart and mind blessed and faithful tranquility, free from all needless and futile disturbance.

Let me be free from the infection of vices. Free me in particular from the vain desire to be recognized, known, loved, and honored by other people. For all those who seek for anything apart from you, my God, are both deceived themselves and deceive others. Direct me to yourself alone, Lord! Release me from the vain desire for the esteem and honor of my fellow human beings. Indeed, let me love or desire no created thing except for your sake alone and in accordance with your divine will and plan.

A prayer for patience in times of tribulation and anxiety of heart

Lord God, my beloved, holy Father, I am not worthy to be visited by you, but rather, I deserve punishment with harsh blows. Since I have sinned and shown myself ungrateful in innumerable ways, I deserve to carry many heavy burdens and to be afflicted with many tribulations. Unlike my good and faithful brethren, I am entirely unworthy to be refreshed by your divine consolations and to be included amongst the guests at your holy banquet.

Nevertheless, I beseech you, holy Father and sweet and merciful Lord, deign to count me as one among your servants. Let me be even the least and lowliest of your slaves so that I may thus be part of your household with all the others, whose footprints I am not worthy to kiss. These have many and great consolations from you. Rightly do you love them, indeed, with a great and special love. For me—who am the least and most wretched of all—it will suffice if you do not spare me from affliction and adversities!

Merciful Lord, may such purifying tribulations be dearer to me than any consolations and pleasures. For these I may suffer solely for your honor, not for my own gratification or for the hope of obtaining any reward. Indeed, to me there is no greater reward and no more precious treasure than to endure trials and adversities for the sake of your honor and glory.

O Lord, who are the highest Truth, pour forth into my heart the radiance of your celestial light! Let me consider myself as an exile in this world, a pilgrim, and an unknown pauper. Let me be as one abandoned and deserted by all things in creation, like one destitute and helpless. Thus shall I seek nothing else but you, my God, and entrust my hopes to you alone.

May I be as one dead to the world and hidden in a tomb, whose very memory has perished without a single trace remaining. Christ, eternal wisdom of the Father, let me contemplate my own condition in such a manner often. Let me be ever mindful of the account I shall have to render of myself at the future judgment and the eternal life to come. Doing thus, I shall prepare myself to appear before your heavenly throne with humble prayers and tears of repentance.

A prayer for knowing and following the way that leads to eternal life

Lord Jesus Christ, you are the true light which is eternal and unchangeable. You humbled yourself to descend into the prison of this world for the purpose of illuminating the darkness of humanity's ignorance and revealing to us the way that leads to our homeland of celestial radiance. In this heavenly homeland, you dwell eternally and shine forth with a glorious brilliance that will never fail nor fade.

O Lord, hear the prayers with which I humbly beseech you, and pour forth into my heart that divine light so that I may recognize and know the path by which I should walk to arrive at eternal life as I make my way through this mortal pilgrimage. May I leave behind all earthly cares and vanities and follow you, my Creator and Redeemer, with the eager step of love until I arrive at the end of this journey. May I persevere in poverty, humility, and patience. May I continue in faith, hope, and charity, and in temperance, chastity, and perfect obedience.

You are the illuminating mirror of life and the lamp of all sanctity. You have gone before me on the way of virtue so that you may lead me to the knowledge of the highest Truth. Once, indeed, I was shrouded in the darkness of sin and error. But you have offered an example of the correct way to live. Even those who do not wish to imitate the example of the saints must at least strive to follow you, for you are the only Lord and the only judge of all. And so that we do not regard this as something impossible to do, you have raised up innumerable good and holy people who have followed your footsteps ardently and faithfully.

Grant to me, O most loving Jesus, the fervor of your spirit. Kindle in me that sacred fire of love, which you came to send into this world.[12] Help me to be animated only with the desire for you and to strive to please you alone. May I never be anxious about being overlooked, disregarded, or neglected by other human beings. Lord, be my highest joy and the true delight of my soul! Abide with me and permit me to abide with you, free from all earthly distractions and liberated from all vain and ephemeral ambitions, aspirations, and fears.

Be my teacher and my master, my creed and my wisdom. As long as I follow you, I shall not fall into any error. If I remain intent upon you, all labors and efforts will seem to me small, all adversities will seem trivial,

---

12 See Luke 12:49.

and all burdens will become tolerable. Imbue me with your love, which has the power to overcome everything. Grant to me genuine humility of heart so that I may not consider myself worthy of anything except whatever your will disposes for me.

O Lord my God, you are my hope and the fulfillment of all my desires! You are my refreshment and the illumination of my heart. I know that you never desert those who hope in you. Sometimes, of course, you permit us to be tempted and tested. But this is only so that we may come to know you more fully and recognize the depth of our need for you.

Jesus, my one beloved, do not desert me in my exile in this world! Be with me always, as you promised. Come to me when I need you most during this time of trial, until the battle of life is complete. And I shall ardently long for the day when you draw me to yourself in your eternal glory, where you—who are truly God—live and reign forever and ever. Amen.

A prayer of salutation to our Lord Jesus Christ

Hail, Lord Jesus Christ, King of all the holy angels! All the virtues of heaven tremble at your commands; all the seraphim and cherubim adore, praise, and bless you forever and ever.

Hail, Lord Jesus Christ, true Messiah and perfect epitome of holiness! You were sent forth from the embrace of the Father into this world. It was you whom the patriarchs longed to behold, and you of whom all the prophets uttered their mystic oracles.

Hail, Lord Jesus Christ, Creator and Redeemer of the human race! It was you whom the apostles and evangelists proclaimed throughout the world as the only Son of God, who was made flesh, suffered, and rose from the dead for the sake of our salvation. In your glorious name, and made radiant with the marvelous power you bestow, these same apostles and evangelists raised up your holy Church unto the very ends of the earth.

Hail, Lord Jesus Christ, invincible warrior, unconquerable hero and most faithful helper of all the saints! It was you whom the glorious martyrs imitated by disdaining all the blandishments of this world and spurning all perils and threats made to body and to life. Such noble souls freely and bravely accepted even death as an undying testament to their unshakable faith in you.

Hail, Lord Jesus Christ, highest priest and eternal shepherd! It is you whom all devout priests, bishops, and teachers of the faith glorify by means of their doctrine and virtue. It is you who inspire the love of holy monks and hermits who walk the narrow way of salvation with complete devotion of mind.

Hail, Lord Jesus Christ, beloved spouse of saintly virgins, consoler of pious widows, hope of orphans, and refuge of the poor! It is you who alleviate the burden of sorrows and who are the eternal salvation of all who believe in you. You are the open door leading to heavenly tranquility to all who draw near to you. It is you whom the innumerable choir of holy virgins, adorned with the radiant beauty of chastity, follow with love and devotion, bearing an immaculate halo of inviolate purity.

Hail, Lord Jesus Christ, light of the world and font of eternal life! You are the true paradise of the soul and delight of the heart. You are the generous giver of all graces, the restorer of innocence, in whom are hidden all the treasures of the wisdom and knowledge of God.

Lord Jesus, to know you is to live. To serve you is to reign. To have seen you but once is to become oblivious of all else. It is you that the glorious host of angels desire to behold and, in contemplating you, find perfect and ineffable bliss.

To you, my Jesus, be all praise and glory, together with the Father and Holy Spirit, both now and forever! Amen.

The Annunciation

DEVOUT PRAYERS

A prayer of love and praise to the Blessed Virgin Mary

O Blessed Mary, most kindly Virgin and glorious Mother of God, of all mortals you alone possess the plenitude of grace and the perfection of piety and love. I implore you to open this treasury of mercy and love to me, your poor and unworthy servant. Pour forth into the depths of my parched soul the gentle dew of the refreshing sweetness which you keep hidden in your most holy bosom. Help me to love ardently and praise devoutly your unique Son, our Lord Jesus Christ, and yourself, most blessed of mothers, with all my heart, all my mind, all my soul, and all my strength. May I pass all the days of my life upon this earth in serving you and your divine Son with true love and fervor of spirit.

O Virgin Mary, golden rose, indescribably sweet and beautiful! Let my prayers poured out to you with devotion enter into the sight of your most holy presence. With these prayers, I knock upon the door of your mystical dwelling place, the most exalted abode within the celestial palace of God. I confide entirely in your mercy in all my tribulations and anguish. For you are the Mother of mercy, and through you each sinner finds their greatest hope of obtaining God's mercy.

Your goodness and mercy immeasurably exceed any praise which mortal lips could ever utter. You surpass the glory and splendor of all the other saints, Blessed Virgin and beloved mistress! By virtue of your sweetness and clemency, you transcend even the angelic creatures. Through your intercession, more than that of any other, the sinner may find the surest and promptest path to the mercy of God. And the spring of your kindness and mercy can never be exhausted, for in your womb the font of infinite goodness—God himself, our Lord Jesus Christ—rested in physical form for nine months.

O beloved Queen, you are the ornament of the highest heaven and the joy and jubilation of all the saints. You are the golden ark of the celestial temple and the delight and hope of the ancient patriarchs. Through your intercession, O blessed and specially chosen

Virgin, divine mercy is promised and bestowed upon all who pray sincerely for the forgiveness of their sins. With you as its faithful helper and powerful advocate, the soul becomes capable of attaining a place amongst the children of God to enjoy unending beatitude and unfettered liberty in the kingdom of heaven.

O most radiant star illuminating the firmament, and gracious Queen of Heaven! There is no earthly maiden or virgin saint who may be compared to your immaculate beauty. For—after your only begotten and divine Son, Jesus Christ—you are the first amongst all the saints and angels and the most perfect of all created beings. God, the eternal Father, knew you before the ages began. In the fullness of time, he created you to be the immaculate Mother of his beloved and only Son. You gave birth to this Son, the Savior of all who believe in him, with unspeakable joy, and thus you shared in the most wondrous miracle of the Incarnation of the Divinity.

Therefore, the whole human race honors and glorifies you with the greatest jubilation. All humanity loves you with intimate and filial devotion. For you, O Mary ever-virgin, are the most beautiful and blessed Queen of all the saints and angels, and the Mediatrix of Mercy to all the world. Every creature in heaven and earth—which God created solely for the glory of his most exalted and holy name—unites to sing your glorious praises, in a sweet-sounding and enthralling melody of endless love. Amen.

A prayer to the Blessed Virgin Mary for her help in the hour of death

O most loving Mother of God, Mary ever-virgin, you overflow with a miraculous sweetness, which the human mind is not able to comprehend or describe! I stand before you now as your lowly servant, humbly bowing before your most glorious throne, which is exalted far above all the choirs of angels in the heavenly kingdom. You have deserved this preeminent rank, O beloved Lady, for you were found to be the most pure and humble amongst all the daughters of Jerusalem. Therefore, your beauty became pleasing in the eyes of God, the divine King; for truly he found no other maiden upon earth who was similar to you.

Again, I prostrate myself before your footstool, eager to praise and extol you with devout lips and a pure heart. Yet I know, chosen Mother of God, that I am not worthy to raise my impure eyes to you. For often have I sinned, weakly succumbing to the lusts of the flesh, the cravings of the eyes, and the pride of life.[1] Indeed, I am unfit to gaze upon your most serene face, radiant with the divine luminance, which fills the whole angelic court of heaven with the most profound admiration and wonder. This face is adorned with lips whose crimson surpasses that of the rose and whose eyes' gentle gleam outshines the stars themselves.

When I consider my own abject unworthiness, I am deeply saddened and filled with frustration at my own impurity. But again, when I recall the multitude of your mercies, I am infused with renewed hope. With you interceding for me and acting as my blessed advocate, surely I shall quickly obtain the grace of forgiveness for my failures and reconciliation to the Lord. What else can I do but see in you, my Lady, my sweetest solace and my most merciful refuge? And not for me only but for all sinners.

Therefore, inspired by the hope of your healing mercy and maidenly gentleness, I fly unto your holy protection, O most gracious of Queens. For, by means of your protection, the weak are given strength and captives receive liberty. Be merciful to me, just as a good Mother. Thus shall I know that you are indeed

---

1 Cf. 1 John 2:16.

the consoler of all who serve you and the most faithful helper of all who trust in you.

Again, I pray to you, Mary, most glorious Mother of God! From now until the final hour of my life, never cease to look upon me with a serene and maternal gaze and a benevolent and loving heart. Hold me in the loving embrace of your arms wherever I may walk during the pilgrimage of my earthly life!

In truth, I do not and cannot know when my final day shall arrive. But when that dark day comes, and when descends the grim and dreadful hour of death which no mortal may escape, please remember me, your humble servant! Stand by my side in the time of my mortal dissolution and lend to my fearful soul all the courage that it shall then so desperately need. Yes, protect it from the foul and unclean demonic spirits which would viciously seize upon it and draw it away to the eternal darkness, to the unquenchable fire and the undying worm! For wherever you are present, O Mary, together with your angelic and saintly cohorts, there the spirits of evil and the demons shall not dare to approach.

By means of your infinitely pure and efficacious prayers, help to reconcile me to your beloved Son, whom I have gravely offended in such a multitude of different ways. After this life—my earthly exile—is ended, take my poor and wandering soul by the hand and lead it through the gates of heaven to the blissful realms of God's star-illuminated paradise. Stand by my side and speak to your divine Son on my behalf. He is, indeed, the omnipotent King of all the ages and the supreme judge of every soul. Yet he once came to you as your tiny guest, announced by the word of the archangel Gabriel, and was held in your embrace and nursed by you, as helpless and mild as any human infant.

By the power of your Son, Jesus, kindly protect and guard me both in life and in death. Grant me the privilege of praising your wonderful name with all the capacity of my heart, my tongue, and my mind. Accept my humble prayer which I pour out to you. Look upon me, most merciful and blessed mother of Jesus, and never forget me.

But I must confess that sometimes I am forgetful of you. Sometimes, I am distracted by fleshly temptations, and sometimes I am weighed down by earthly worries and duties. Yet I hope that you, for your part, will not forget me. For you offer your mercy to all who venerate and love you, even if they do so only imperfectly.

Hail, O most blessed Virgin Mary! I greet and venerate you upon bended knees; to you I bow my head in devout adoration; to you I join my hands in ardent thanksgiving and gratitude. And, so that you may deign to hear my humble prayer, I shall now dare to speak to you that angelic and immortal salutation by which God himself magnified your glory, just as your soul magnified his:

Hail Mary, full of grace! The Lord is with thee.
Blessed art thou among women, and blessed is
the fruit of thy womb, Jesus. Amen.

A prayer to the Blessed Virgin Mary imploring her special consolation

Receive, O most merciful Mother of God, your servant who flies to you in the midst of tribulation! Receive me, most pure of virgins, like a forsaken orphan, who has no one else to offer consolation. My Lady, see my affliction and open to me your heart of deepest mercy. Lo, I stand at your door knocking, crying out and begging for you to open to me! And I shall not withdraw, I shall not depart, until you grant me kindly admittance.

I know of your incomparable sweetness. I know of the maternal tenderness of your heart, which is replete with a love divine in nature and origin. And therefore

I flee to you often, both when things are going well for me and when I face tribulations and difficulties. For you never fail to provide me with motherly consolation and encouragement, and to refresh and renew my spirit. With you speaking words of solace to me, what need have I ever to feel sad? And with you as my protectress and guardian, how shall any enemy harm me or ever dare to approach me?

Most kindly Mother, turn your ears to my humble supplications. Noble maiden, grant to me to drink of your font of refreshment, and pour out to me the pure waters of your super-abundant grace. How very much I need your grace during this present time of struggle, and indeed at all times in my life! And never shall I become weary of your guidance, protection, and assistance.

So delightful and potent is your grace that a single drop of it, descending upon my lips like dewfall, is more precious to me than all the world. Compared to you, everything else in this life seems inconsequential and trivial. You are wonderfully generous in your gifts and marvelously sweet in your words. In your womb, the highest Wisdom of God dwelt in the flesh. The Holy Spirit consecrated you, the mighty archangel Gabriel saluted you in jubilation and homage, and the power of the Most High himself overshadowed you!

O Mary, refresh me with your teachings of piety and wisdom. Speak to me but a single word, and my soul shall be consoled. Certainly, I ask of you no difficult or impossible thing, my Lady. Utter to my heart but a single word of solace, and I shall be filled with unspeakable joy and gladness.

Behold, I flee to you in my hour of need! Receive me with a kindly and serene countenance, and bestow upon me your encouragement and soothing mercy. By this alone shall I know that my humble service and devotion has not failed to find favor in your sight.

Come to me, dearest Mary! Bring with you your mellifluous ointment with which to anoint my heart in its tribulation. For you know perfectly how to alleviate the pain of an aching heart, and how to restore it to happy tranquility. Come, most merciful Mistress, with the ever-new graces of Christ! Hold out your holy right hand to raise me up, your servant who lies fallen before you. Come, chosen Mother of God! Reveal to me the solace of your endless mercies. For, as you can see, I am almost annihilated and virtually reduced to nothing by my troubles. And yet, I do not forget you, my Queen; nor shall I ever forget you, as long as time endures.

Come to me, my beloved, my hope, and my joy! For whilst I converse with you in the raptures of prayer, all goodness is present to me and all wickedness and trouble departs far away. How desirable and how delightful it is for me to hear the voice of the Mother of my Lord Jesus Christ! But what are the words I seek to hear from you? They are none other than those revered and awesome words once spoken by your divine Son to the blessed apostle John, when he said: "Behold, your mother!"[2]

He heard these words from the Lord, but I, with a devout mind and ardent spirit, seek to hear them now from you, my Mistress. Say to me: "Behold, I am your mother! Here I am, standing before you." When I hear these words, my soul will revive and I shall rejoice in your presence, like a small, lost child who has just found his longed-for mother.

Let your loving voice penetrate into the ears of my heart, and let your sweet utterance bear with it all the consolation of the Holy Spirit. My heart shall then assume a new and fresh faith. My fears shall vanish, and doubts will touch me no more. The dark clouds of despair that surround me shall be dispelled as mist by a

---

2 John 19:27.

ray of golden sunlight at the sound of those words I so long to hear, "Behold, your mother!"

My soul, hold firm to this commendation! Embrace the blessed Virgin Mary. Embrace the Mother of God, together with her infant Son, the Lord Jesus Christ. Give thanks to her always, for she never fails to hear the prayers of those who cry to her in distress, and she never leaves them without consolation. She indeed is the Virgin who bore God himself to the world, the mystic branch growing from a royal tree, from which sprang forth the divine lily—Jesus Christ the Lord, the King and Savior of the universe! To him be glory and honor forever and ever. Amen.

A prayer to the Blessed Virgin Mary in times of distress

Hail Mary, full of grace! The Lord is with thee, O most serene Virgin.
Hail, you who are the special hope of the needy!
Hail, kindly Mother of the orphan!
Often have I known dark and difficult times—

when all the doors of heaven seem to be shut to me . . .

when it seems that my sins have alienated me from God . . .
when my firmness of mind fails completely and my resolve becomes feeble . . .
when I can find succor and solace in no earthly thing . . .
when I am consumed with such tedium that nothing in this world delights me . . .
when my heart seems to be bound up in chains of anxiety . . .
when it seems that the sun of joy has given way to the tempestuous night of fear and sorrow . . .
when all my consolations have been replaced with desolation . . .
when the gales of temptation rise against me and assail me . . .
when unexpected weakness overtakes me . . .
when foes and adversities seem to surround me from every direction . . .

At such times, to whom should I turn to but you, O Mary? To whom should I flee but to your maternal protection; for you are indeed the most kindly refuge of the poor, sorrowful, and afflicted. Who or what can lead me safely to the tranquil harbor of salvation, except for you? For you are, in truth, the most beautiful and splendid Star of the Sea, whose gentle but refulgent light never fails nor conceals itself from those who earnestly seek it.

O Mary, sweet and beloved Mother, you are that most brilliant star which illuminates all those who raise their eyes to you in prayer and supplication. To you, therefore, I flee today and humbly implore your assistance! For I know that whatever you request of your divine and obedient Son, you shall easily obtain. If you are for me, O glorious Mistress, who can be against? If you bestow something of your grace upon me, what foe shall I fear?

Extend to me your protecting arms, that I may hasten to your loving embrace! Say to my soul, "I am your advocate. Take courage and do not fear. As a mother consoles her son, so shall I console you!" Such indeed are your gracious utterances, your words of unsurpassable sweetness. Who will grant to my heart to hear such words without cessation?

How sweet is the speech from your mouth! Speak, my Lady, to the heart of your servant, for I long to hear you! For I am indeed your servant and the servant of your Son. If you are a mother to me, then the Lord Jesus Christ is most truly my Brother. And you bore him, the Son of God, not only as your own beloved infant but as Savior of the whole world.

There is no other maiden who is similar to you in virtue and beauty, nor in charity and mercy, nor in piety and sweetness. You have no equal in faithfulness and maternal gentleness, nor in compassion and clemency. Therefore, this day I choose and assume you as my special protectress. This day, I faithfully pledge myself to your service and consecrate my heart entirely to your love. And not merely for the duration of this present life but for all eternity. And it will suffice for me as consolation to know that I am now inseparably bound to you by this dedication. Behold, already I rejoice and am wonderfully encouraged by you. From henceforth, never shall my heart cease to sing the praises of your most sacred name!

O how beautiful and lovely you are, holy Mary, filled with every grace! To number all of your virtues and merits would be like counting every single star in heaven. And just as the heavens are high above the earth, so your life was exalted above that of other mortals, and the splendor of your glory above the hosts of angels. My humble prayer now ascends to you, my Lady, so that you may plead my cause in the presence of your holy Son. For before your Son, who is also Son of God, there is no one who is able to stand justified by their own merits alone. O most clement Queen, to you I confess openly my sins and failures and will reveal all the hidden impurities and blemishes of my soul. I know the greatness and potency of the virtue that proceeds from you, which will bring sure healing and solace to my sorry heart.

How sweet is the name of Mary, a name that carries the anointing of a specially privileged grace, a name always to be spoken with the utmost reverence and veneration. O heavenly and angelic name, which the evangelist so carefully and piously entrusts and commends to the faithful: "And the name of the Virgin was Mary."[3]

O sacrosanct and most laudable Mary! You are indeed the door of heaven, the portal of eternal life, the temple of God, and the sanctuary of the Holy Spirit. Whatever I see in created things which is noble and beautiful, whatever I consider in the lives and merits of the saints which is great and virtuous, I wish to offer and dedicate to your splendor and glory. For it is truly worthy that I, together with all creation, should extol with perpetual praise you, O Mary—whom I now choose as my special Mother and most faithful advocate, to the

---

3 Luke 1:27.

unending glory and honor of your blessed Son, Jesus Christ. Amen.

A prayer on the great virtues and merits of St. John the Baptist

Most holy and illustrious saint, John the Baptist, you were a special friend of our Lord Jesus Christ and a most faithful forerunner of the Lord! O beloved and venerable patron, you were great in this earthly realm but are now even greater in the kingdom of heaven, where you splendidly illuminate the choir of saints with your special honor and refulgent virtue! For you were truly the greatest of all the prophets and have primacy amongst the holy patriarchs. Though you were the last to be born of this noble company, you take precedence over them all by the glory of your merits and the radiance of your goodness.

Just as the brilliant star of morning is the brightest of all the stars of the night and heralds the coming of the sun, so you prefigured and announced to the world the coming of our eternal King, the Sun of Justice and Son of God, the Lord Jesus Christ. Your birth was foretold by the archangel Gabriel; you were sanctified by God prior to your birth. Even then, you were filled with the Holy Spirit of prophecy so that you leapt within your mother's womb when you heard the sound of the Blessed Virgin Mary's voice. You returned the faculty of speech to your father who had been rendered dumb. And with this voice, he proclaimed, "You, blessed child, shall be called a prophet of God the most High!"[4]

Thus you came to be born in a most marvelous fashion. But more wondrous yet was your mode of life. For at the age of seven, you left your parents' home and entered the desert.[5] There, unsupported by any human consolation, you lived an angelic life. You lived in complete solitude, poverty, and silence, until the day you returned to preach to the people of Israel. You embarked on a most difficult course and set yourself an arduous rule of life, content with the crudest of food and drink, and firmly declining all the luxuries of the rich and powerful. Inspired by the Holy Spirit, you proclaimed to the people the coming of salvation and the way of moral rectitude. You urged the crowds to repent and seek after the coming kingdom of God.

It was you who proclaimed the advent of the Lamb of God himself, our Lord Jesus Christ. This Lamb of

---

4 Luke 1:76.

5 Presumably the source of this is some apocryphal writings, or a traditional belief.

God you prefigured by your own way of life—your fidelity, courage, justice, and righteousness. And when the Lord was present in the flesh, you pointed him out physically, declaring to the crowds, "Behold, the Lamb of God! Behold him who takes away the sins of the world!"[6] And, O great and venerable John, exhibiting the most profound reverence and awe, you baptized with your own hallowed hands Jesus Christ, the living Lord and only Son of God, in the waters of the Jordan.

At that time, you heard the sublime voice of the Father, saying, "This is my beloved Son, in whom I am well pleased."[7] You beheld with your own blessed eyes the Holy Spirit descending upon and hovering over the head of the Savior in the form of a dove. Thus you witnessed the ineffable mystery of the Trinity, through its own celestial revelation and its own glorious heavenly manifestation. And it was you who bore witness to the true light of the world, Son of God, our Lord Jesus Christ.

And Christ bore witness to you also and declared the magnificence of your sanctity and virtue. He said of you something which no other prophet or patriarch

---

6 John 1:29.

7 Matthew 3:17.

has ever merited to hear: "Of all those born of women, no man greater than John the Baptist has arisen."[8]

O John, you were the prototype and model of all martyrs. For, fervent with zeal for justice and love of chastity, with a courageous voice you reprimanded the incestuous marriage of the wicked king Herod. Because of the unbending constancy of your faith, you were then cast into a foul and gloomy dungeon and patiently bore the heavy chains of incarceration. At last, at the request of a most reprehensible woman who thirsted for your blood, you gave up your blessed head to be savagely severed off by the executioner's sword. And this was the same blessed head that had been consecrated by the infant God!

Thus you were decorated with robes of royal purple, colored with your own noble blood, and received the victor's palm of glorious martyrdom. And thus as a lamp which had shone forth into the world, you entered triumphant into the celestial court of the holy patriarchs and prophets. And, despite your cruel death, you were certainly filled with overwhelming and undiminished joy at the advent of the Savior of the world and Redeemer of the human race. For he was the one

8 Matthew 11:11.

you foretold and pointed out. He was the one whom you preceded, in your birth, baptizing, preaching, manner of life, and fearless death.

O most sublime and exalted of holy men! How could I possibly ever succeed in worthily praising and extolling your tremendous virtues? I find you so rich and great in all aspects of sanctity that you seem to stand out with particular splendor amongst the whole choir of saints. Rather, indeed, because of the superlative brightness of your splendor, I am hardly able to gaze on you at all! And neither may I ever sufficiently admire your singular dignity.

Everywhere your name is heard, and in each church, the praises of St. John the Baptist ring forth. If I seek you among the angels, I find you with them as their peer and companion, for you were rightly said by Christ to rank above all holy men who were born of mortals.[9] If I seek you among the company of prophets, I find that you are, in fact, more than a prophet—again as Christ declared.[10] If I seek you among the apostles and evangelists, I find you ranking first, as you were the first to be named as "the voice" of the Good News, "the voice

---

9 See Matthew 11:11.

10 See Matthew 11:9.

of one crying out in the wilderness."[11] If I look for you among the ranks of virgins, I find that you were a true and chaste virgin throughout your entire life of celibacy and abstinence. If I look for you among the holy monks and hermits, I find that you were an earnest cultivator of solitude and silence, and the exemplar for all generations of monks. If you are sought among the innocent and pure, there was never a man who was more innocent or more pure than you. And if you are sought among those who devoted themselves to a life of penitence and abstinence, you take primacy of place for your austerity of life, stricture of morals, and integrity of conscience.

O most holy man, praiseworthy in all things! You were beloved by God, venerated by angels, and admired by human beings. O burning and brilliant light of the omnipotence of God, illuminating the earth and making heaven rejoice. You converted sinners, encouraged the just, raised up the fallen, and strengthened those who were firm in their faith. Thus you drew all people to God, making straight the path in their hearts for the One who would show the way of salvation and open the gates of heaven.

---

[11] Matthew 3:3.

Remember me, O great saint! By your prayers and intercessions, obtain mercy for me from the just Judge of all sinners. Sow in me the seeds of virtue so that I may be liberated from the hold of all vices. With you as my protector, may I merit to receive the anointing of the Holy Spirit and enter through the gates of perpetual beatitude after the struggles of this life. O great pillar of the kingdom of heaven, help me in the hour of my death! Be my advocate before the King of Angels, and speak a favorable word on my behalf. Although my own faults and failures weigh me down and burden me, let your merits raise me up and be a shield defending me against the foe. When my soul leaves behind the shackles of this mortal body, let me be aided by your glorious merits and virtues, and so pass safely and securely to the eternal palace of celestial beatitude. Amen.

A prayer on the privileges of love of the blessed Apostle John

Hail, St. John, gentle and noble apostle! Hail, most exalted of all the Evangelists! Hail, faithful guardian of Mary, the Mother of Jesus! I salute you with the devout reverence of my soul. I honor you out of the depths of my heart. I invoke you with affectionate sighs and prayers. I sincerely desire to extol your praises, to describe your virtues, and to relate the magnificence of your works. Most pious and chaste Apostle, permit me to speak well of your glories!

You were the disciple who is described as being especially beloved by Christ. The Lord Jesus called you while still young from becoming married to this world, to be the spouse of holy and pure celibacy instead.[12] He freed you from the bonds and allurements of the flesh and filled you with every heavenly charism. For the love of Jesus, you left your earthly father in the boat with his nets to follow your divine Father.[13] You tirelessly proclaimed the Gospel of the kingdom of heaven. Wondrous signs and miracles testify to your sanctity. You did not fear persecutions and afflictions but embraced them all with unflinching and heroic courage.

You were among the chosen, inner group of apostles who ascended Mount Tabor with the Lord Jesus Christ.[14] There, the radiant glory of the transfiguration

---

12 According to ancient traditions, St. John is singularly identified among the apostles as being unmarried and a virgin and was believed to be the youngest of the apostles. He is also traditionally identified with the "beloved disciple" of the Gospel according to John.

13 See Matthew 4:21–22.

14 See Matthew 17:1–8.

was manifested to you. There, in mystic ecstasy of mind, you heard the sublime voice of the heavenly Father declaring Christ to be the true Son of God. Thus the stupendous arcana of the mystery of the divine filiation of Jesus and his perfect divinity were opened to you.

O holy and blessed Apostle, how many were the secrets which Jesus revealed to you—truths which the fallen human mind is not able to grasp or comprehend! Therefore I ask you, beloved John, pray for me with all your fervor. Pray that I am able to relinquish all worldly vanities and temptations. Ignite my heart with the saving mysteries of Jesus, upon which you were so ecstatically intoxicated. Let me spurn earthly deception and ascend with you the mountain of virtue unto the clear heavens of purity and innocence.

For all the fleeting vanities and ephemeral pleasures of this passing life—which people seem to prize so highly—are, in truth, really nothing. It was to demonstrate this that Christ, the eternal Wisdom of God, showed to you the glowing vision of the ineffable future glory to be given to his saints.[15]

And as his blessed passion drew nigh, it was you he sent, together with Peter, to prepare the paschal feast,

---

15 See Revelation 21.

the supper of the Lamb. At this holy supper, the Lord humbled himself as a servant to wash your feet and those of the other disciples and thus left an immortal sign and example of love and devout humility.[16] O venerable John, who at the royal banquet of eternal life, lovingly reclined upon the breast of your revered and adored Master.[17] You are the beloved disciple who, while at that forever-remembered supper, asked Jesus, "Lord, who is it that shall betray you?" And Christ, as a sign of his loving intimacy with you, confided, as if in secret, "It is he to whom I give the piece of bread which I shall dip into the dish."[18]

O truly privileged and specially chosen Apostle! Amongst the noble company of apostles, you were blessed with a singular grace of chastity, and hence were found worthy of a particular familiarity with the Lord. Thus to you were revealed profound mysteries which remained hidden or only dimly perceived by the others, as if by an intimate word of divine knowledge uttered in your ear.

How many were the arcane wonders which you drew whilst reclining on the breast of Jesus! The words of your Gospel fill the entire earth, transmitting like a flowing,

---

16 See John 13:1–15.
17 See John 13:23.
18 John 13:24–26.

crystal stream the celestial doctrine you drew from the chest of the Savior. I beseech you, O beloved Apostle, refresh my thirsting soul with the sweetness of your divine eloquence. Make me to be present with you at the supper of the Lord! Let my heart take delight in the beauty of Christ's discourse to his disciples, the words of which you so faithfully recorded in your Gospel.

You, blessed John, were among the disciples as they followed Jesus through the Kedron Valley.[19] You were among the privileged three who accompanied the Lord to his secret place of agonizing prayer in the Garden of Gethsemane.[20] And you did not fear to accompany Jesus, captive and bound, into the palace of the high priest.[21] It was sincere love for Jesus which compelled both you and Peter to follow him more boldly than did all the others. But when human frailty and weakness caused Peter to deny him and to flee at his hour of death, you remained faithfully at his side.

Most holy Apostle John, with perfect and unwavering loyalty, you followed Jesus, cruelly wounded and condemned to the cross. With tearful sorrow, you accompanied the Blessed Virgin Mary and Mary

---

19 See John 18:1.

20 See Matthew 26:37.

21 See John 18:15.

Magdalene, who were almost overcome by grief. You stood by Jesus with unshakable fidelity while he hung in agony from the cross, and by the side of the Blessed Virgin as her heart was pierced by the sword of pain. In this is shown the insuperable power of the holy love which burned within you as a celestial fire.

For this reason, with his dying breath, Jesus specially commended his Mother to you, that you should henceforth serve her as your own mother. O most faithful and chaste guardian of the Blessed Virgin Mary, protector of the Spouse of the Church, treasury of the eternal kingdom! You were chosen to be, after Jesus himself, a second son to the Mother of God. To you was entrusted the Ark of the Covenant and the mystic door of paradise, through which the King of Glory had entered the world. Such indeed was the wondrous privilege enshrined in those words of Christ, "Behold, your Mother!"[22] Thus the Mother of God became your own mother, the Mother who is blessed in all eternity. To you was she committed; to you was she entrusted.

O, who will grant to me to have such a Mother as the blessed Virgin? Who will grant to me such a noble and loyal guardian as St. John, the beloved disciple?

---

[22] John 19:27.

Who will appoint for me such potent protectors and guides to defend my poor soul against the enemy when the terrible time of death draws nigh?

Most good and merciful Jesus, remember me in my final hour. When my own physical voice and senses of the body fail me, may the prayers of your blessed Mother and St. John strengthen me.

O Mother most merciful, Mary ever-virgin, I ask you, through your divine Son and through the apostle whom he commended to you from the cross, help me in every time and place, but most of all when I am in distress and struggle.

Blessed and beloved St. John, faithful friend and merciful guardian, protect me with the aid of the celestial army and with the invincible sign of the holy cross. Repel from me the devil, that wicked enemy of each Christian soul. In the name of Jesus, set me free from all fear when the grim hour of death approaches.

O Blessed Mary and St. John, you two noble saints are truly as two beautiful and ever-fruitful olive trees.[23] With the utmost humility, devotion, and earnestness, I commend myself to your intercession and protection. Defend me, I pray, from all perils and foes, and lead me

---

[23] Cf. Revelation 11:4.

safely and happily to dwell with you and all the saints in the eternal kingdom of Christ our Lord. Amen.

A prayer of praise to St. Thomas the Apostle[24]

Hail, Thomas, glorious apostle, worthy of the highest praise and honor!

Hail, illustrious preacher of the evangelic truth, and light and splendor of all the Church!

Hail, fervent lover of Christ, who had the unique privilege of touching his most holy side.[25]

Hail, illuminated contemplator of the very depths of the truth and profound visionary of the Trinity.

Hail, enlightener of humankind, who converted the mighty kingdom of India to the faith by means of your wondrous miracles and wise teaching.

Hail, worker of astounding marvels, who raised the dead to life, cleansed lepers, illuminated the blind, put demons to flight, and cured every affliction in the powerful name of Christ!

---

24 The particular devotion to St. Thomas the Apostle exhibited in this prayer and the following one perhaps reflect the fact that this saint was the namesake, and therefore a special patron, of the author.

25 See John 20:27.

Hail, noble architect and heavenly builder, who, in place of an earthly palace, built for the king of India an eternal mansion in heaven.

Hail, zealous advocate of chastity, extoller of virginity, and most devout venerator of the priestly dignity.

Hail, you who spurned riches but gave alms with a liberal hand, supported the poor, and built up the Church with energy and piety.

Hail, most patient sufferer of persecutions, indefatigable laborer for the salvation of souls, and committed pastor of all the faithful!

Hail, strong and dauntless hero of the faith, conqueror of demons, destroyer of idols, corrector of error, victor over tyrants!

Hail, St. Thomas, noble apostle who endured and overcame the scorching flames, and finally, driven through by a sword, gave up your life for the love of Christ in glorious martyrdom. Amen.

A prayer on the merits and virtues of St. Thomas the Apostle

O St. Thomas, my venerable and beloved patron and chosen disciple of Christ, hear the prayers which I pour out to you. Through my daily supplications, I seek your glorious protection and support. Listen favorably to me and show your generosity and care to my heart, and I, for my part, shall never cease to praise you with new and daily-increasing devotion. My heart burns in prayer, and in my meditation, the fire of divine love is kindled. In veneration of your holy name, all my inner being is filled with the most sweet jubilation.

You were indeed a specially chosen disciple of Christ, and you are also especially loved by me. For I have chosen you as a particular patron and advocate, and committed my entire life and soul to your protection and guardianship. You are, indeed, able to achieve much with your Master, the King of Glory. Therefore I beseech you to be mindful of me, a sinner. By your holy intercession, help to reconcile me to my merciful Creator. You were eternally pre-known and chosen by God the Father. In time, you were called by the only-begotten, incarnate Son to partake in the apostolic order. This you fulfilled with courage and fidelity, spreading the Gospel to the very ends of the earth.

Christ himself instructed you in the mysteries of the faith and strengthened you with his own mellifluous and divine eloquence. The physical presence of the Lord filled your soul with gladness, and you witnessed with your own eyes the stupendous wonders and miracles which he performed. And the Lord imparted to you also the power of curing the sick and casting out demons.

Having left all things, you followed Jesus ardently and embraced the way of poverty and humility with a joyful and committed heart. With Jesus, you patiently endured condemnation from the Jews and the hatred of those who love this world more than God. Accordingly, it was you who expressed your readiness to be stoned and to die with Christ to your co-disciples when you said, "Let us go and die with him!"[26]

At the Last Supper, you partook of the sacramental feast as one of the guests at a royal banquet. There you received, with the greatest reverence and faith, the true body and blood of Christ, the perfect pascal Lamb of redemption, from his very own sacred hands. By participating in this supper, you were consecrated for the celebration of this great Eucharistic mystery by the High Priest himself, Jesus Christ, and thereby ordained for all eternity as a bishop and pastor of faithful souls.

Our Lord also humbled himself to wash your feet, giving you an example of the greatest humility and teaching by this mystery the necessity of washing one's soul from all worldly contaminations. When Christ

---

26 John 11:16.

predicted his betrayal, passion, and death, you were struck with the most grievous and heartfelt sorrow. It was you who declared yourself ready to suffer and die with your divine Master. In this, you expressed the spirit and fervor which animated the whole company of apostles. And although this was denied to you at the time, later you consummated this desire in the glories of your own martyrdom.

It was you who asked the Lord as he uttered his sweet words of consolation at the Last Supper, "Lord, we do not know where you are going, so how can we know the way?"[27] How much fervor and faith, how much loving determination to follow Jesus, is expressed in this question! And the Lord responded with his immortal utterance, "I am the way, the truth, and the life. No one comes to the Father, except through me."[28] What a sublime and wonderful answer your question merited, O Thomas, and thereby gave to the world! How profound and sacred the mystery which you first heard from the Lord! Indeed, Christ revealed himself to you as the way to the Father and showed himself to be one with the Father in divinity and essence. And he thus

[27] John 14:5.
[28] John 14:6.

manifested himself to be the eternal life to all those who love him.

You accompanied Jesus to the Mount of Olives.[29] On account of the bitterness of your sorrow at Christ's death, you were not present when first he appeared to the other apostles on the third day, resurrected from the tomb. Yet, for your sake, he appeared again gloriously on the eighth day and made to you a special and particular revelation of his humanity.[30]

At that time, he showed to you the physical signs of his victorious passion. He invited you to touch the most sacred wounds on his hands and on his side, and thus expelled from your heart any remaining trace of doubt or disbelief. How blessed you are, Thomas, to have touched the wounds of Christ! How indescribably great and sweet was the grace you drew from contact with these wounds! Out of this touch, you recuperated your faith in the bodily resurrection of Christ and received thereby a new hope of mercy and more ardent love for the Savior. By touching the wound in his side, you were perfectly reconciled to him, and by touching the wounds in his hands, you were totally sanctified and united to Christ in the most intimate way possible.

---

29 See Matthew 26:30.

30 See John 20:24–29.

Out of the open side of Christ, divine love flowed into you, and out of his sacred wounds, certainty of his glorified humanity was infused into your heart. Out of your doubts, you emerged more strongly convinced, firmer, and more profoundly enlightened.

Indeed, Thomas, let no one think that the doubts which you experienced harmed you or reflect badly upon you. For out of these doubts, greater certainty was given to you, and greater certainty was given to all believers. O strong and unshakable column of the company of apostles! You strengthened our faith by procuring for us such wonderful signs. You assist the faithful who implore your intercession, you obtain mercy for all afflicted by infirmities, and you provide a wonderful example for all who find their faith wavering or uncertain. You teach those who suffer from doubts that they should never despair, and you raise them up and console them by your own example.

Blessed Thomas, you are the inviolable shield of our belief; you are the firm anchor of our faith, a radiant lamp of charity, a clear mirror of purest chastity, an exemplar of perfect justice, and the splendid light of virtue. O glowing illuminator of the Church, filled with the balm of celestial grace, how fragrant and sweet are the words of your blessed profession of faith!

For you proclaimed Jesus to be truly God and truly human when—as you touched the side of your beloved Master—you declared, "My Lord and my God!"[31]

Most sweet and beloved are these words, overflowing with faith, delightful to hear, and wonderful to meditate and pray upon. You were totally seized in divine rapture and inebriated with celestial love when you drew these mysteries from the wounded side of our Redeemer. It was these mysteries which you expressed in that immortal and ineffably sweet declaration, "My Lord and my God." How perfect and potent was the balm you found in the open wound of Christ! How utterly wonderful was the glorious taste you drew from the mellifluous stream of eternal wisdom!

You are blessed, O Thomas, and blessed was the speech of your mouth, for it revealed to us the mystery and the price of our eternal redemption, through the passion and Resurrection of Christ. In the suffering and death of Christ is our healing and redemption. In his resurrection is our eternal life and our unending glory. You became a truthful and bold witness to this Resurrection, just as Joseph, the spouse of Mary, was a faithful guardian of and witness to her virginity. He

---

[31] John 20:28.

was commanded to accept the Blessed Virgin as his wife. You were commanded to touch with your own hands the sacred flesh of Christ. After the vision of an angel, Joseph became a reverent guardian of the Virgin Mary. You, after touching the wounds of Christ, became a faithful advocate and evangelist of the Gospel of salvation.

When Mary Magdalene, filled with love, sought to touch the Lord, she was firmly prohibited from doing so. But Christ not only did not prevent you but rather commanded you to touch him! He did this in order to impart greater certainty and clarity both to your faith and to the faith of the whole Church. Yet although he invited you to touch the wounds in his hands and his side, he did not invite you to touch the wounds in his feet. Why was this? Perhaps it was to teach reverent prudence in the desire for signs and assurances. For you were truly filled with faith and all your doubts were dispelled as soon as you saw your resurrected Master. Yet your touching of him was necessary for the sake of instructing and assuring others of the veracity of the mystery which you first proclaimed—that Jesus truly is our Lord and our God. O blessed Apostle, to whom fell the privilege of receiving and articulating this recognition of the glory and divinity of Christ!

Thomas, you were present with Peter and John and two other disciples when you went fishing on a boat on the Sea of Tiberius.[32] There, you saw the Lord standing upon the shore. Following his instructions, you cast out your nets again and captured a tremendous haul of fish. Embarking on the shore, you shared a meal with Jesus, accepting bread and fish from his hands, and were thereby joyfully refreshed.

Along with the other apostles, you witnessed the Lord as he ascended into heaven in glory to be seated at the right hand of the Father. You saw two angels clad in robes of brilliant white who spoke of the second coming of Christ, and you heard their wondrous prophecy: "Just as he has gone, so will you see him come back from heaven."[33]

After the ascension of Christ to the glory of the Father, you and the other apostles returned from the Mount of Olives with great joy and went to the upper room where the Last Supper had been celebrated. It had been in this same upper room that the resurrected Lord had appeared and that you had touched his sacred wounds. With Mary, the Mother of God, and the other apostles, you waited patiently in this upper room for the

---

32 See John 21.

33 See Acts 1:6–11.

coming of the Holy Spirit. During this time of waiting, you shared in the insistent prayers and loving recollections of the deeds, words, and virtues of Christ. On the great day of Pentecost, you received the Holy Spirit as a tongue of living fire and were filled with knowledge of the languages and tongues of all the people of the earth. You were imbued with all celestial charisms and ignited with the flame of invincible faith. Thus armed with the spirit of fortitude and wielding the shield of patience, you overcame the threats and persecutions of priests and potentates, of princes and prefects. In obedience to God, you chose to suffer many hardships and to undergo imprisonment and death rather than to be silent from the proclamation of the Good News.

Inspired by the Holy Spirit, you sowed the seed of the Gospel in many lands and regions. At last, after a vision of Christ, you went to the most remote nation of India. There you acquired abundant fruit for the Lord, through the conversion of vast multitudes of people, demonstrating the truth of your teaching by an abundance of miraculous signs and wonders.

According to the dispositions of Divine Providence, you met in India the three holy kings of the East, or Magi, who had visited the infant Christ, led forth by the prophetic star. And you related to them all the details of the life, death, and resurrection of Christ. Once they had been reborn through the sacrament of Baptism, you then consecrated them as priests of the Lord. As a devout pastor, you established many churches throughout India, ordaining priests to celebrate the mysteries and to teach the faithful.

Finally, after a long and laborious life of impeccable virtue, ardent zeal in evangelization, generous care for the poor, and countless miraculous healings of the sick, you merited to enter into the eternal rest of the blessed. There you enjoy the splendid vision of the divine glory in the eternal mansion of the heavenly Father. Thus was fulfilled the prayer of Christ before the hour of his arrest and the commencement of his passion: "Father, I wish that those whom you have given to me, shall be with me where I am, so that they may see the glory which you have given me."[34]

Rejoice, O Thomas, blessed apostle, for you now sit at the table of Christ in the kingdom of his heavenly Father. Never again shall you drink the imperfect and tainted wine of this earth, never again shall you know death; for now, the time of your persecution has passed. The night of trial is over and the powers of darkness

---

[34] John 17:24.

are reduced to nothing. Now the ruler of this world has been cast out.[35] And he lies, conquered, under your feet. He and his foul tyranny have been overthrown while you, exulting, are crowned in heaven! Now, you shine among the apostolic choir as a radiant star of the celestial firmament. Now, you share the supernal beatitude of the triumphant company of white-robed martyrs. Now, you enjoy the rewards of your labors, together with the countless crowd of people whom you converted to the faith, and thus saved from the grasp of hell. Now, as a mighty warrior, you enjoy the glories of a magnificent victory!

Holy Mother Church rejoices with you and gives solemn thanks to God for the splendor of your virtues and heroic sanctity. The people of India celebrate with special devotion in the presence of the remains of your mortal body. But all Christians throughout the world are strengthened and protected by your intercession.

Hail, glorious apostle Thomas! By your intercession, obtain grace for your servants. In the hour of our judgement, stand faithfully by us as our advocate, together with the glorious Virgin Mary. And may the blessed

---

[35] Cf. John 12:31.

fruit of her womb—our Lord Jesus Christ—be praised and adored forever and ever! Amen.

Collect 1

O God, you appeared to blessed Thomas, your apostle, after your resurrection, and invited him to touch the scars of your wounds. Grant to us, supported by his prayers and intercession, to hold the wounds of your passion in our minds faithfully so that we may follow your holy footsteps and merit to come to the glory of your resurrection; who live and reign forever and ever. Amen.

Collect 2

Lord Jesus Christ, illuminator of the world and giver of eternal life, at your Last Supper, you answered the question of your blessed apostle, Thomas, with the proclamation, "I am the way, the truth, and the life."[36] Through the merits of this same apostle, grant to us to ascend from the humility of your humanity to the majesty of your divinity and to be made sharers at the eternal banquet in your heavenly kingdom; who live and reign forever and ever. Amen.

---

[36] John 14:6.

Collect 3

O God, you sent your blessed apostle Thomas to preach the faith to the people of India and distinguished him by the glory of a multitude of miracles. Grant to all the faithful, who implore his intercession, to be found unwavering in belief and effective in good works. Through our Lord Jesus Christ, your Son, who lives and reigns with you in the unity of the Holy Spirit, God forever and ever. Amen.

A prayer on the great and special privileges of St. Mary Magdalene

Hail, blessed Mary Magdalene, great and beauteous saint! You were specially chosen and called by Christ, and he bestowed on you many unique signs of divine familiarity and affection. I venerate and praise you. I humbly invoke you, and I love and embrace you with the sincerest devotion!

For Jesus, who is the eternal Love, loved you very much and elevated you to the heights of the celestial firmament. You are that noble and famous saint about whom the holy Gospel relates so many wonderful things, which are instances of your piety and sanctity.

In you, the sinner sees the hope of forgiveness and the righteous person sees the privilege of the anointing of grace from Christ, the font of all divine mercy. You are described as having once been a sinner, but now you possess a thousand-fold happiness. For the Lord gazed upon you from heaven and converted your tender but erring heart. Thus you were drawn to repentance with a spirit that was truly humble and contrite. And, having been forgiven and consoled, you were a sinner no more, but a most ardent lover of Jesus Christ!

You, Mary, are that penitent and tearful woman who, in a wondrous act of devotion and adoration, washed the feet of the Lord with your tears and dried them with your hair. You covered these sacred feet with your loving kisses and anointed them with most precious ointment. Thus you offered to the merciful God a great and beautiful oblation, fully commensurate with the magnitude of your previous sins. And the Lord accepted this offering of your penitence most graciously, saying, "Your sins are forgiven you,"[37] and "Your faith has saved you, go in peace."[38]

How sweet and overflowing with mercy are these words, and how filled with grace! They are indeed to be

---

37 Luke 7:47.

38 Luke 7:50.

longed deeply for by every repentant sinner. O heavenly Healer, although you are the most exalted and holy of all beings, in mercy you did not refuse to be touched by the hands of a sinful woman.

Rejoice, therefore, Blessed Mary, to have received such a marvelous abundance of God's clemency. Pray for me and for all sinners, who have fallen into the pit of iniquity. Grant that the Divine Mercy may save us from the jaws of Leviathan, that malign and ancient serpent, and restore us to safety!

O Mary, you became a specially blessed and pious woman. Following the Lord through towns and villages, you served with your own resources the one who is the Creator and giver of all things. Thus it was that you and your sister, Martha, received Christ as the welcome guest at your house. When she was solicitous and anxious with care for serving his material needs, she complained that you were not helping but merely remaining still in his presence. But the Lord responded on your behalf—as he often had done before—commending your stillness more highly than Martha's solicitude and busyness. "Mary has chosen the better part," he said, "and it shall not be taken away from her."[39] I ask you, O happy and celestial Mary, make me share with you this "better part" so that after all the labors of this mortal life, I may arrive at the wonderful rest of eternal contemplation.

Mary, you are also the loyal and loving sister of Lazarus, whom our Lord and Savior caused to rise up from death.[40] Christ was moved to compassion by your tearful prayers and those of your sister. He himself shed tears for his deceased friend, thereby showing how truly and authentically he was united to our human condition. I implore you, O Mary, beloved friend of Christ, request on my behalf the gift of divine grace. For such grace is indeed the true life of my soul. May I be granted both to live and to die in God's saving grace, and thus to share in the glory of the future resurrection with you and all the saints!

O Mary, you are like a fragrant ointment of sanctity! For you anointed the feet of the Lord Jesus a second time in the house of Simon the leper. With your customary devotion, you generously poured most precious balm upon his sacred head as he reclined at the feast.[41] At that time, the whole house was filled with the scent

---

39 Luke 10:42.

40 See John 11.

41 See Matthew 26:6–7.

of this rare ointment. Today, the entire Church is filled with the fragrant perfume of your precious virtues. Would that I, an unworthy sinner, could deserve to be anointed with a little of this marvelous scent in the interior chamber of my heart! Then every foul stench that is within me because of my sins would be driven out to be replaced with the sweetness of your merits.

O Mary, you were a tireless imitator of the passion of Christ. As our Lord carried his cross, you followed him closely through the gates of Jerusalem. All the while, you shed tears of the bitterest sorrow at the thought of his suffering and the impending and ignominious death of a man who was completely free from the stain of sin. Your suffering was increased also by the sight of the pain and anguish of the Blessed Mother of Jesus. How willingly you would have carried a cross in the footsteps of your Lord had it been permitted to you!

And when Christ had been raised up in his glorious but dreadful crucifixion, you stood at the foot of the cross together with his Blessed Mother and the beloved apostle, St. John. As he was laid in the tomb, fresh waves of sadness arose in your heart. O, how bitterly then did all Christ's friends mourn his tragic but noble death, but how especially poignant was the lament from the holy women! But those who wept most passionately of all were those who loved him more than any others—that is to say, the Virgin Mary, his most holy Mother, and you, Mary Magdalene, his most devout and adoring disciple.

I am a sinner and like a branch which is dried up and withered. Who will give to me a flowing fount of tears whereby I may join with Mary Magdalene in loving and ardent weeping for the passion of my Lord Jesus Christ? O Mary, hear my prayers, and grant that I may learn to weep such tears of piety and compunction with you! O holy and radiant Mary, you visited the tomb of the Lord with devout fervor, arriving before the rising of dawn with spices for burial.[42] There you beheld holy angels, who gave testimony to the resurrection of the Lord. But to see angels of the Lord did not suffice to you, unless you could see also the Lord of angels.

Therefore you stood outside the tomb, sunk in deepest lamentation.[43] For you believed that your beloved Master had been taken away. But, O Mary, weep no longer! For, lo, the Author of life has arisen! And it is you who will be the herald of the glory of the Resurrection. In this we firmly believe, and in believing, we glorify God through you! The risen Jesus himself appeared to you in that garden. What ineffable joy was

---

42 See Luke 24:1–8.

43 See John 20:11–18.

then yours! And it was your singular honor to be the first to announce this Good News. Thus you became truly the apostle of the apostles.

I humbly prostrate myself before your feet, O Mary, and beg that you intercede for me and for all who love and venerate you and share in your rejoicing at the privileges and gifts by which the Lord glorified, blessed, and exalted you. O happy Mary, merciful patroness, remember me now and at the hour of my death. May your merits and prayers help me to obtain reconciliation and forgiveness when my soul departs from the body to appear in the presence of almighty God. Amen.

Collect

O God, you received the repentance of blessed Mary Magdalen with mercy. After her many sins, you bestowed upon her an even greater fullness of forgiveness. Through her intercession, grant to us to shed tears of true penitence for our sins and, having repented, to be filled with hope for your mercy, which shall lead us to life everlasting. Amen.

A prayer on the virtues and merits of the most noble virgin, St. Agnes[44]

Rejoice, St. Agnes, virgin of Christ, who ardently loved Jesus while you were in the world!

Rejoice, St. Agnes, meek virgin, who pleased God by the goodness of your life!

Rejoice, St. Agnes, gem of chastity, whose radiance shall never fade nor grow dim!

Rejoice, St. Agnes, whose beauty was such that no one else in the world could ever equal it!

Rejoice, St. Agnes, most lovely rose, whose death was precious in the eyes of the Lord, and who ascended to the heights of heaven!

O most sweet and holy Agnes, I implore your mercy, I dedicate myself to your love without reserve, and I commend myself devoutly to your efficacious prayers. Hear your servant crying out to you, filled with an earnest desire to serve you. For I love you with a sincere heart and shall ever declare your praises.

---

44 St. Agnes, a Roman virgin and martyr of the third to fourth century, was the patron saint of the house of Canons Regular, where Thomas lived and spent most of his religious life.

In you, I find all that I love. In you, I discover all that I long for. In reading the story of your life and martyrdom, I encounter everything I admire and everything that is worthy of praise.

You are the mirror of chastity, the beauty of virginity, the splendor of faith, and the adornment of the house of God.

You are the glory of the angels, the exemplar of sanctity, the lover of the devout, and the guardian of the pilgrim.

You are a nurse to the sick, the dispeller of vices, the voice of encouragement to the languid, and the daughter of the apostles.

You are the companion of the martyrs, the sister of virgins, the honor of widows, and the patroness of the celibate.

O most meek, humble, and devout virgin! O prudent, innocent, and chaste maiden! O radiant and celestial saint, pure from all earthly contamination! You cared not for gold, nor for riches, nor for illustrious lineage, nor for possessions, but preferred the love of Christ to all the things which this world has to offer. In return, Christ held you as one most dear to him and chose you as his spouse while you were still an infant. You were of a noble Roman family by birth but shone with an infinitely more splendid nobility by virtue of your faith and modesty.

It was your love of Christ which impelled you to undergo the horrors and torments of fire and the sword. But to you it was a sweet thing to die for your beloved Christ. For his holy angels stood ready to take your precious and innocent soul and to carry it on wings of love to the joys of paradise! Thus you entered the bridal chamber of your heavenly spouse, beautifully adorned with the victor's palm of glorious martyrdom.

O holy Agnes, I beg that you should ask Christ, your spouse, to grant to me health of mind and body. May he help me overcome all the temptations of the devil, to control the desires of the flesh, to escape from the distraction of worldly vanities, and to avoid bad company. May he direct me along the good path of his commandments and allow me time for repentance for my sins and the amendment of my life.

May the Lord grant me forgiveness for all my sins and pour into my heart the consolation of the Holy Spirit. May he help me to abstain from all bad thoughts and actions and to strive after that which is truly good. May he mercifully permit me to arrive at a peaceful and holy death and prepare for my soul a secure passage to fly to its celestial dwelling place. And may he command his holy angels to lead me into his hall of eternal beatitude. There, in company with all the saints, may I gaze forever upon the face of God's eternal glory, in heaven's supreme joy which knows neither alteration nor end. Amen.